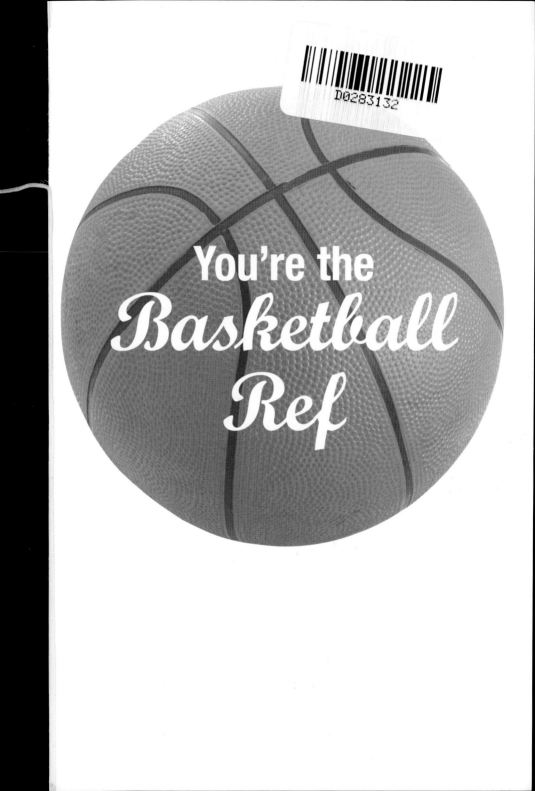

You're the
Basketball
Ref

You're the
Basketball
Ref

Mind-Boggling Questions to Test
Your Basketball Knowledge

Wayne Stewart

Skyhorse Publishing

Skyhorse Publishing books may be purchased in bulk at special discounts for sales promotion, corporate gifts, fundraising, or educational purposes. Special editions can also be created to specifications. For details, contact the Special Sales Department, Skyhorse Publishing, 307 West 36th Street, 11th Floor, New York, NY 10018 or info@ skyhorsepublishing.com.

Skyhorse® and Skyhorse Publishing® are registered trademarks of Skyhorse Publishing, Inc.®, a Delaware corporation.

Visit our website at www.skyhorsepublishing.com.

10 9 8 7 6 5 4 3 2 1

Library of Congress Cataloging-in-Publication Data is available on file.

Cover design by Qualcom
Cover photo credit: Associated Press

ISBN: 978-1-510743-335
Ebook ISBN: 978-1-510743-342

Printed in China

CONTENTS

INTRODUCTION

First of all, I have a confession to make. I am not nearly as fascinated by the rules of basketball as I am by the odd plays of the game (which, admittedly, do tie in with the rules). As a young man, it took me quite some time to get the "over and back" rule straight, and strange plays such as the one involving Larry Bird in Section Two do evoke a "wow" or a "What's the rule on that one?" from me when I run across them. Many unusual plays also leave me waiting for the refs to iron things out and for the television announcers to clarify matters.

By the way, an odd play I witnessed back around 1968 involved a player being handed the basketball while he stood out of bounds, ready to inbound the ball at the next blow of the ref's whistle. Moments later, to the amazement of everyone on hand, the player did not pass the ball to a teammate but instead took a step forward and began to dribble the ball onto the court as if he were playing a one-on-one game of playground basketball. Needless to say, there's a rule against that—no need to quiz anybody on *that* one.

Still, from the time I saw that one peculiarly foolish play during a JV game held in my high school's bandbox gym in my hometown of Donora, Pennsylvania, I *have* been quite interested in the rulebooks for various levels of basketball play.

There are, in fact, as you'll soon see, rules for just about everything that can occur on a court. You should be aware, too, that because the basketball knowledge of the readers of this book must surely encompass a wide range, I've sprinkled some questions in that may be easy for some of you. Likewise, to challenge more sophisticated fans of the game, some questions may come off as being too difficult for other readers. Please feel free to simply skip any question that doesn't suit your taste.

However, before breezing through too many questions, you must be aware of another factor. In many cases, the question and answer may not even be the most interesting part of some of the items in this book. On some occasions, a question will lead to a somewhat tangential matter. Yes, the hope here is that you'll do well on the rule questions, but that you'll also find yourself saying, "I never knew that," from time to time about some extra material that goes beyond the actual questions. For instance, one scenario pertaining to a given rule could involve, say, a John Wooden-led UCLA team or player, and after the answer for that particular question is revealed, you might be presented with some bit of trivia about Wooden and/or his program, or perhaps a biographical note about this or some other legend of the game.

Therefore, this is not merely a quiz book, as it has several purposes beyond merely testing your knowledge of basketball rules. Other goals include informing/educating you (e.g., for all you aspiring refs—did you know that through 2012, there were 13 referees enshrined in the Hall of Fame, such as Earl Strom and Marvin "Mendy" Rudolph, to name a few?) and, in some instances along the way, even entertaining you. Good luck!

NBA REFEREES: (FROM LEFT TO RIGHT) KEN MAUER, TOM WASHINGTON, AND STEVE JAVIE

BRIEF BASKETBALL BACKGROUND

Before moving on to the quiz, here is, as TV's Lieutenant Columbo used to say, "Just one last thing." This is a bit of basketball background, a sort of prequiz, layup drill—or call it your warm-up prior to game time. See how much of this chapter's information you already knew.

As a basketball fan, you probably already are aware that Dr. James Naismith is given credit for the creation of basketball, unveiling his now-famous 13 rules of the game (more on them later) in January 1892. Naismith was a 30-year-old physical education teacher at a YMCA facility in Springfield, Massachusetts, who was looking for an indoor sport that would occupy men during the bitter New England winter. He was assigned the task of thinking up such an activity and was given a mere two weeks to accomplish this. He came up with his gem, a game he felt was "easy to learn and easy to play in the winter by artificial light," with one day left before his deadline was to expire.

You may also know that Naismith later coached the Kansas Jayhawks, registering an embarrassing 55–60 record there over nine seasons as well as the lowest winning percentage (.478) in the history of that program . . . ironic "achievements" from the man who was the father of the game.

However, did you know, as our first trivia aside, that the first college to organize a team was Geneva College in Beaver

Falls, Pennsylvania? That happens to be the hometown of Hall of Fame quarterback Joe Namath. Shortly after Geneva got its program up and running, several other colleges followed suit, including Iowa in 1893, Ohio State and Temple in 1894, and Yale the following year.

The first game ever known to be played in public was in 1892; it was a contest held between students and teachers at a YMCA training school in Springfield, Massachusetts. That's also, quite appropriately, the location for the Naismith Memorial Basketball Hall of Fame. The students, by the way, won their 30-minute game over the faculty by a score of 5–1 (you have to wonder what the spread and the over/under were on that one). Some 200 spectators saw Amos Alonzo Stagg come through with the lone score for the teachers. Stagg would go on to become a member of both the football and basketball halls of fame. His football fame began on the gridiron as an All-American at Yale.

In the earliest of basketball contests, such as the 5–1 affair or the first known women's intercollegiate contest, a 2–1 decision played back in 1896, dribbling was not yet a significant part of the game.

Initially, the peach baskets were nailed to a balcony (some sources say a running track), which ran around the gym that Naismith used . . . and the balcony just "happened to be 10 feet off the floor." Those baskets were replaced shortly by "15-inch cylindrical wire baskets." For the record, the rim is now 18" in diameter, while the ball is 9" across. Furthermore, soccer balls were first used before basketballs were put into play in 1894 under Naismith's guidance. The following year, backboards were added, which, among other things, prevented "fans from interfering with play," as the baskets were frequently hung on the previously mentioned balconies.

Scoring rules were different, as well. In 1896, for example, a field goal was changed from being worth one point to the current two-point value. Free throws, which had been good for three points, became only one point.

It is believed that the first professional game also occurred in 1896 in Trenton, New Jersey. The teams consisted of former YMCA players, a logical connection to Naismith and the roots of the game.

* * *

A new century brought additional evolution to the game. The concept of playing a five-minute overtime period rather than ruling games that ended in regulation play as a tie didn't come into play until 1908, two years after rims with open nets "began to replace the peach baskets." However, the boring requirement of holding a jump ball after every score, a practice originally necessitated by the old peach baskets, was abolished for the 1937–1938 college and amateur seasons.

It wasn't until 1909 that glass backboards were approved. That same year, a new rule read that a player would be disqualified from a game after he committed his fourth personal foul.

Even the very name of the game has gone through a change. Originally the sport was spelled "basket ball," and there were nine players per side going at it for two 15-minute halves. It wasn't until 1921 that the spelling became "basketball."

As the game evolved and players' skills and size increased, new rules had to be written up. Interestingly enough, there have been more than just a few occasions in which a new rule came into effect due to (or *largely* due to) the influence of one man—more on this in the quiz sections.

There is no question that of all the major sports played in the United States, baseball is the one that hasn't required numerous rules changes over the years. In fact, at one point, some baseball people seemed almost obstinately proud that their game had little reason to change—baseball was, after all, the national pastime. Of course, one reason baseball's rules were, by and large, without much need for change is that it is our oldest game and any ironing out of significant rules (how many balls outside of the strike zone to a batter will result in a base on balls or how far from the mound should home plate be) were taken care of long, long ago. Until recently, for many years, it could be stated that the last major rule change in baseball was the adoption of the designated hitter, which occurred in 1973.

By way of contrast, football constantly seems to tinker with its rules, often attempting to rev up the offense or to curb the chaotic, violent nature of the game. Basketball, too, has seen its share of rule changes in the not-too-distant past. It can certainly be argued that basketball has instituted or changed more major rules due to, as mentioned, the influence or actions of one man than any other sport. Names such as George Mikan and Wilt Chamberlain come to mind, but again, more on this later.

 With all that in mind, it's time to whet your interest and wet your whistle—it's your turn to make the call.

SECTION TWO

NBA/ABA RULES AND SITUATIONS

For the purposes of this book, the words referee and official will be used loosely to mean those men whose duties are to run the game, call fouls and violations, and so on. Technically speaking, a referee, for example one working a high school game, has duties other officials don't have, such as checking the books, giving the pregame speech to team captains, and tossing the ball up to begin the game. We won't worry about any distinctions here. Let's get started.

(1) A player is leaning out of bounds while in possession of the basketball. He's got nowhere to go but out, and he has nobody open to pass the ball to. Off balance, he decides his only recourse is to shoot the ball, even though his position on the baseline means he has to arch the ball up over the rear of the backboard at just the precise, seemingly impossible angle to make it drop softly into the hoop. If the shot should fall, would it count?

Answer on page 29

(2) Let's say Michael Jordan, who, as difficult as it is to believe, was not good enough to make his high school varsity team as a sophomore (he had to settle for playing JV ball then), is dribbling the ball near the three-point arc a few strides away from the top of the key when he suddenly

spots a seam and, putting on a burst of speed, makes a dazzling move. He drives toward the key, picks up his dribble, and then clearly takes three strides to the hole with the first step being a quick, maybe even choppy, cutting one, just microseconds after ending his dribble. He then caps off his play with a patented windmill dunk. What's your call here?

Answer on pages 29–32

(3) Picture Hall of Famer (Class of 2011) Chris Mullin back in the days when he was with the Golden State Warriors. The left-handed shooting Mullin is dribbling the ball as he races down the court at breakneck speed. He stops dribbling and leaps forward, landing on both feet at the same time. Has he just traveled—after all, when he quit dribbling, he did, in effect, take two steps, that is to say, both feet and legs traveled forward before he landed—or was his maneuver legal?

Answer on page 33

(4) Chris Paul has possession of the ball when he takes a spill. He never lets go of the ball as he rolls on the floor. Is this a traveling violation?

Answer on page 33

(5) Imagine Kevin Durant takes a jumper from about 14 feet out, and, just for the sake of this unlikely scenario, he comes up empty, missing the rim and backboard entirely. Hustling after his shot, he is somehow the first player to get to the ball. He then:

CHRIS PAUL

A) tries to take a quick follow-up shot or

B) tries to tip the ball in.

Are either or both of these second attempts illegal?

Answer on pages 33–34

6 Like Jordan, Allen Iverson was also said to have gained an unfair advantage at times by doing what should be, according to purists, whistled as an illegal move. The elusive guard frequently did this when he employed his quickness, some say especially on his first step, to execute a killer crossover step en route to the hoop. What violation did he (and, to be fair, others in the NBA) "allegedly" commit on more than a few occasions?

Answer on page 34

7 Hall of Famer Adrian Delano Dantley, at 6′ 5″, was a tiny power forward who poured in 23,177 career points. He really liked to study things over before shooting his free throws—and he went to the line a lot. As a matter of fact, through 2011, only ten men ever attempted more lifetime foul shots than Dantley, who clicked on .818 of all his free throw attempts.

He had a rather odd habit—or perhaps call it a ritual—that he displayed at the charity stripe. Before actually shooting the ball, the man called "A. D." would roll and spin the basketball around a bit. At times it even seemed as if he were caressing the ball. All of his rituals lead us to this question: Let's say the ref has handed the ball to Dantley as he toes the line, ready to shoot a free throw. Is there a rule limiting the amount of time he now has to release the ball—if so, do you know how long he has to shoot the ball in this situation?

Answer on pages 34–37

(8) Imagine a player who, just before shooting from the foul line, hesitates for a split second—say he has a sort of hitch to his shot. Would a slight hesitation as described, or a full-fledged fake shot, a sort of pump fake at the line, be considered illegal?

Answer on pages 38–39

(9) Here's an odd one from March 2, 1962, the night Wilt Chamberlain scored his record 100 points in a single game, held in Hershey, Pennsylvania, of all places. With his 100th point already in the books and with just 46 seconds left on the clock, two free throws by New York Knicks forward Willie Naulls made the score 169–147, a new record for the most total points scored in an NBA contest. When the clock wound down to a tick or so under the 12-second mark, the Knicks quickly fouled Joe Ruklick of Wilt's Philadelphia Warriors, rendering him unable to get the ball to Chamberlain to do even more damage. Ruklick went to the line, and then, in a sort of stage whisper, informed Wilt the Stilt that he was about to purposely miss his second shot, hoping that Chamberlain could grab the rebound and score yet again.

Referee Willie Smith overheard Ruklick's intentions

and took immediate action. Under the rules, what could he do here?

Answer on pages 38–39

(10) Similar question: Let's say Chauncey Billups, whose career free throw percentage hovers right around the .900 mark (.894 through the 2011–2012 season), is at the line in late 2011. His Los Angeles Clippers trail by two as he prepares to shoot his second foul shot. Time has nearly expired, so, in a dire situation, he decides to miss the free throw, then follow his shot, rebound it, and stuff it back in with a game-tying dunk. He fires the ball off the backboard and, sure enough, executes his plan to perfection. Is he doing anything different from what Ruklick had planned on doing? Have the rules changed? In short, does his score count?

Answer on page 39

(11) Back to the 100-point onslaught of the unstoppable 7′ 1″ Chamberlain. This colossus of the hardwood rarely felt comfortable at the free throw line—he'd wind up with a career free throw percentage of just .511—but for one magical night, he hit on a staggering rate of .875 of his foul shots. For that matter, he was on fire from *everywhere* that night, connecting on 36 of 63 shots from the field.

Throughout his career, Chamberlain was well aware of his woes from the foul line. Due to this, he experimented with different styles of shots, including one-handed, two-handed, a jump shot from the free

WILT CHAMBERLAIN

throw line, shooting from three feet behind the line, a fall-away shot, and the method he used the night he rained down 100 points, granny or underhand style—the very same style that Rick Barry, a career .900 (#3 all-time in NBA play through 2011) free throw artist, has always insisted is the best way to sink foul shots.

Late in the 100-point game, the Knicks were over the limit of six team fouls, putting the Warriors in the bonus situation. What exactly was the "bonus" for a team back then when they went to the line?

Answer on pages 39–48

(12) It's the 1953–1954 season, and the Fort Wayne Pistons win the opening tipoff in a game versus the Minneapolis Lakers but cannot get off a shot within 24 seconds of gaining possession of the ball. What would the call be here?[1]

Answer on pages 49–51

(13) Here's a quick yes-or-no question: When the NBA drew up its first set of rules in 1946, was it legal for teams to play zone defense?

Answer on page 51

(14) Initially, were players permitted four, five, or six personal fouls before they were disqualified from further play in a given game?

Answer on pages 51–52

---

[1] Hint: It's a trick question.

15 True or false: Let's say the Knicks and Celtics were playing a game during the 1950–1951 NBA season, which wound down to the final three minutes. At that point, a jump ball took place after a free throw had been made. The two players jumping were the man who had just committed the foul and the player who had been fouled.

Answer on page 52

16 True or false: During the 1953–1954 season, a player who was charged with three personal fouls in a given quarter had to sit on the bench for the rest of that quarter.

Answer on page 53

17 What is the current distance from the outer edge of the three-point line to (the center of) the hoop in the NBA?

Answer on page 53

18 What was so unusual about the regulation basketball used in the old ABA (American Basketball Association)?

Answer on page 53

19 True or false: If any part of a player's foot is on the baseline or the sideline, refs are to treat this situation as if that player were entirely out of bounds.

Answer on page 53

20 Guess within two years the first time the NBA used three referees in a game rather than two.

Answer on page 53

21 Guess within 5 feet the required length and width of NBA courts.

Answer on page 53

22 When Rick Barry was acquired by the Houston Rockets, he was asked what jersey number he wanted to wear. Because #24, his number since his days in high school, was already taken by Moses Malone, Barry asked if he could wear #2 for home games and #4 when the Rockets were on the road. Was this permitted?

Answer on page 54

23 Yes or No: Is it legal for a player to boost a teammate up— to help him jump higher in an attempt to dunk the ball?

Answer on page 54

24 Yes or No: Is it legal for a player to grab the rim to hoist himself up a bit to, let's say, dunk the ball?

Answer on page 54

25 What would you do if a player somehow caused "the ball to enter the basket from below"? Say a player tipped the ball in such a way it first went through the net from underneath the iron and then passed by the top of the rim before finally falling back through the hoop—what's your call?

Answer on page 54

26 The year is 1972, and you're working a game between the Atlanta Hawks and the New York Knicks. Pistol Pete

Maravich is, just for the sake of this imaginary scenario, camped out in the lane and looking to take a pass from teammate Sweet Lou Hudson. The play breaks down, and Maravich realizes he may soon be called for a three-second lane violation, so he steps out of bounds directly under the hoop and then steps back into the lane. Does he now have an additional three seconds in the lane before he must once again exit that area?

Answer on pages 54–57

(27) In Major League Baseball, a team may protest a decision made during a game if the umpires made a mistake involving rules (not judgment). If the protest is upheld and the team that filed the appeal went on to lose the game, the contest must be replayed, picking up the play at the exact moment of the protest. Does the NBA have such a provision?

Answer on page 57

The next ten questions deal with what nba.com calls the league's "misunderstood rules." Fill in the blank with one or both of the conditions we're looking for in this question regarding the defensive three-seconds rule.

(28) A man playing defense is not permitted inside the key for more than 3 seconds unless _____.

Answer on pages 57–58

If everything in the following item concerning goaltending is basically correct, simply put "True" as your answer, but if even one part of it is way off target, you must pin-point the incorrect information.

(29) True or false: A defensive player is not allowed to touch the ball on a shot after it has reached its apex—if he does, the shot counts. Nor can a man playing defense touch a shot after it has made contact with the back-board and is headed toward the rim, whether or not the ball is headed up or down. If the basketball is on or right above the rim in the imaginary cylinder, nobody from either team is permitted to touch it—if a defender breaks this rule, the basket counts; if a player from the offensive team touches the ball, no points can be awarded on the play.

Answer on pages 58–59

(30) True or false: A defender is allowed to use an extended forearm to the back or the side of the man with the ball in order "to maintain his legally obtained position" when he is "outside the lower defensive box" (the LDB is "the area from the bottom tip of the free throw circle to the endline between the two 3' posted-up marks") and "below the free throw line extended."

Answer on page 59

(31) True or false: A defender is permitted to "momentarily touch an opponent with his hand anywhere on the court as long as it does not affect the opponent's movement," which includes his balance, rhythm, speed, or quickness.

Answer on page 59

32 When an NBA game is under the 2:00 mark in the fourth quarter or overtime, there is a rule regarding certain fouls. For instance, what is the penalty if a defender commits a foul before the basketball is released on an inbound pass?

Answer on pages 59–60

33 Flagrant fouls are, by definition, "unnecessary and/or excessive," and there are two classifications of them in the NBA, with the more serious of the two being not only unnecessary, but also excessive. At any rate, what is the penalty for any flagrant foul?

Answer on page 60

34 True or false: NBA refs are trained that "contact which is incidental to an effort by a player to play an opponent or to perform normal defensive or offensive movements should not be considered illegal."

Answer on pages 60–62

35 Yes or no: Is everything in the following sentences correct as far as NBA rules are concerned about the fumbling of the ball?

A player picks up his dribble then fumbles the basketball. He is allowed to recover it without being guilty of a turnover: "If his pivot foot moves to recover the ball, he must then pass or shoot the ball. If he fumbles and recovers it without moving his pivot foot and before the ball touches the floor, he retains his status before the fumble. Therefore, when a player jumps to shoot and the ball slips out of his hands, he may recover the ball."

Answer on page 62

36 Define the basics of illegal picks and screens—just what makes them illegal?

Answer on page 62

37 List the basic points that a ref must consider when determining if a blocking or a charging foul should be called.

Answer on pages 62–64

38 Imagine Oscar Robertson bringing the ball up the court when he suddenly dribbles the ball so high that it bounces over his head. What's the call here?

Answer on pages 64–65

39 Imagine that you've been assigned a game between the New York Knicks and the Detroit Pistons back in January 1977. Earl "the Pearl" Monroe of the Knicks glances up at the shot clock and realizes that, with just 2 seconds showing on that clock, he must heave up a shot. Detroit's Howard Porter barely gets a piece of the ball, which then falls out of bounds. How much time will the Knicks have to get off another shot? Is it:

    A) 2 seconds
    B) 5 seconds
    C) 10 seconds
    D) 24 seconds

Answer on page 65

40 Let's say that Lou Hudson fouls out of a game back in the 1972–1973 season and his Atlanta Hawks coach Cotton Fitzsimmons is fuming over the call. He argues with the refs and then, perhaps out of spite or frustration, takes his good ol' sweet time putting a replacement for Hudson into the game. He better not fool around too long, though, because this was the first season for a new rule that stated there was a definite time limit for getting a replacement for the disqualified player into a game. How much time was allotted for such a change?

Answer on page 65

41 True or false: Decades ago, the NBA had a rule (instituted in 1977–1978) that stated that a player was to be fined $25 for hanging on the rim during warm-ups before contests began.

Answer on page 65

42 True or false: Prior to the 1977–1978 season, it was not legal for a player, following a missed foul shot, to attempt to score without first returning to the floor with a rebound.

Answer on page 65

The 1977–1978 season was a busy one for those who drew up NBA rules. Here are some others:

43 During the final two minutes of regulation or overtime, a team signals that they want a timeout, doing so right after they gained possession of the ball. Under the rules of the day, they were then given an option of putting the ball in play from one of two spots when play resumed. Name those spots.

Answer on page 66

(44) A player is fouled but gets kicked out of the game before he can take his free throw(s). He was, by rule, to "immediately leave the court and one of his teammates on the floor be designated" to shoot in place of him. Who picks the player who goes to the free throw line?

A) his coach
B) the opposing coach
C) the refs

Answer on page 66

(45) A player scores a field goal but does so in the wrong basket on a shot that the officials believe was unintentionally made by the shooter (i.e., a pro hoops version of a Roy "Wrong Way" Riegels or Jim Marshall play in which football players ran in the wrong direction with the ball). What is the ruling on such a bizarre occurrence?

Answer on pages 66–67

REFEREE MATT BOLAND

ANSWERS

1. As peculiar as the shot in this question is, it actually happened in an NBA game. Larry Bird took and made the shot, which, given his spot on (almost *off*) the court, the angle he had to release the ball from and the touch he had to put on the basketball, made it perhaps the most famous Bird basket that didn't count. The refs waved off the shot as illegal.

   Bird was always known for his dexterity—actually, make that ambidexterity. Anytime he found an edge in switching the ball to his off, or left, hand, he could and would do it; and he made quite a few shots using that advantage . . . and some from a pretty good distance from the rim.

   One sportswriter covering the 1981 NBA All-Star Game in Cleveland's old Coliseum was initially surprised to see Bird signing autographs with his left hand. Then, after taking a moment to reflect on all the times he'd seen Bird shoot lefty, the surprise quickly wore off.

2. Let's think a moment here. Legendary superstar Michael Jordan takes three steps? What's the call? Nothing. At least that's what cynics say. Of course, a glance at the rulebook over the years indicates the call should be traveling and a turnover.

   The plaintive shout of "The refs let him get away with traveling" is probably the biggest gripe purists have when it comes to NBA refs. Of course, if a fan's favorite

**LARRY BIRD, GUARDED BY
KAREEM ABDUL-JABBAR**

player "gets away with it" to complete a highlight reel play, that's a different matter.

For the record, here's a look at just a few of the things the NBA rulebook (Rule #10, Section XIV) has to say about traveling: First of all, a player who gets the ball while he is standing still is permitted to pivot, using whichever foot he establishes as the pivot foot. Now, if a player wants to dribble the ball after a pivot foot has been established, he must be certain the ball has left his hand before he lifts his pivot foot off the floor. If a player has the basketball and he does raise his pivot foot off the floor, he has to shoot or pass the ball prior to having that pivot foot return to the floor.

There's much more in the rulebook concerning traveling, but let's just go with a simple example. Say a player has, as Jordan did in the question, completed his dribble. He is permitted to "use a two-count rhythm" after that before shooting the ball (or passing or coming to a stop).

Sometimes players' feet are so quick that it's difficult to determine if they took a step right after or immediately before giving up the dribble—did he really take more than two strides? you wonder. In our scenario, three steps is more than a two-count. Blow your whistle if you can take the heat from Jordan et al.

Still, it seems the question persists as to whether or not NBA players such as LeBron James earn frequent travelers' miles. You make the call, but the thinking here is, they certainly do. That's just the way the game is played, and the greater the player (or so it seems to many, perhaps *most* observers), the more he makes out like the proverbial bandit. In 2009, according to sportswriter Brian Windhorst, "The NBA has rewritten another long-standing rule that directly benefits James and surely will kick off a debate with basketball purists. It is now in writing that players are permitted to take two steps after they 'gather' the ball and not be called for traveling." Windhorst quoted the rule, "A player who receives the ball while he is progressing or upon completion of a dribble may take two steps in coming to a stop, passing or shooting the ball." Windhorst pointed out that the rule, which he referred to as the "LeBron James Rule," was simply making official what had "become common practice for years."

Some critics would also say that the league should get tougher on players who travel because men of NBA caliber don't need help to excel. Jordan, for example, didn't average 30.1 points per game (ppg.), the highest average in the annals of the league, and a lifetime total of 32,292 points just because he got away with some violations. Then again, even the most severe of critics wouldn't want to watch many games if refs got so tough on making calls that tons of the stars, the players people pay to watch, were, say, fouling out of games left and right.

The bottom line is probably this: The game of basketball is a wonderful one, and your ultimate choice is to take it, even with its obvious warts, or leave it—most of us choose to accept and appreciate it for what it is.

3 What Mullin did here is called the jump stop, and it is considered to be a legal move under NBA rules. Basically speaking, Mullin completed his dribble by employing "a two-count rhythm in coming to a stop." He not only loved using this move, but he was flat out great at it, and more than just a few of his nearly 18,000 lifetime points scored in NBA play came on pretty shots off the jump stop.

In the same article in which Windhorst wrote about the "LeBron James Rule," he stated, "By the letter of the law, players executing the jump stop must land on both feet at the same time and then may establish a pivot foot by taking a step." He pointed out that the very strong and quick players such as James can frequently "use the jump stop as an extra step, landing on one foot and then with the second foot before taking yet another step as his pivot. James executes the move so quickly and smoothly that he can 'get away with it.'

4 The key to this question, one dealing with an often misunderstood rule, is the last part of the following sentence paraphrased from NBA rules. If a player hits the deck while he is holding onto the ball or while he is coming to a halt, he will, by rules, be called for traveling *if he gains an advantage* by rolling on the court.

5 Yes, these second field goal attempts by Durant are both considered to be traveling violations. It is a turnover any time a player who has just taken a shot from the field

becomes the first player to touch the ball after his shot did not touch the rim, the backboard, or another player. He may not, for example, grab his own air ball rebound for a stick-back or for an attempt to tip the ball into the bucket. By the same token, if a player should drop the ball while he is in midair, he is not allowed to be the first player to touch the ball.

The rulebook also states that after traveling violations are called, the other team gets the ball, which is to be awarded to them at the sideline and at the spot closest to the violation, *but* no closer to the baseline than the foul line extended.

(6) Whether you were taught to use the phrase "palming the ball" or "carrying the ball," any way one looks at it, the act of placing one's hand underneath the ball during a dribble (a sort of cupping of the ball while on the run) and then turning/rotating the ball over on the next dribble is illegal. One sportswriter said that, in effect and technically speaking, once the player cradled the ball, his dribble stopped, so when he next took a dribble—say, while making the crossover step—he was guilty of double dribbling.

(7) As the NBA rules state, "Each free throw attempt shall be made within 10 seconds after the ball has been placed at the disposal of the free-thrower." Most players take at least a few seconds to get situated, take a breath, and set their sights on the rim, but rarely is the time limit a factor.

Rarely, but not always.

DWIGHT HOWARD

In April 2011, Dwight Howard, who at the time was a member of the Orlando Magic, was going through his lengthy free-throw routine when Boston's Gerald Henderson "made a show out of counting out the seconds" of Howard's motions, which includes a hitch as he releases the ball. The refs made the taking-too-much-time call, took away his free throw shot, and infuriated Howard so much that he threw the ball "toward the corner of the baseline, earning his 18th technical foul of the season."

Howard, a notoriously poor free throw shooter, broke a record held by Wilt Chamberlain for almost 50 years when he went to the line 39 times in one game. He sank 21 of those shots in that January 2012 game in which the Golden State Warriors "hacked Howard intentionally throughout" the Orlando 117–109 win.

By the way, on January 4, 1984, Dantley went 28-of-29 from the foul line to tie the record for the most free throws made in a game, tying Wilt Chamberlain, who, almost miraculously, shot 28-of-32 on the night he pounded home 100 points. On two other occasions, Dantley shot 26 for 27, meaning he owned three of the five best single-game point totals from the foul line.

He also shares the record for the most foul shots made in one quarter, with 14. He led the NBA in free throws five times and is number seven all-time for free throws made. In short, he drew fouls the way a magnet attracts iron filings, often employing deadly, deceptive head and pump fakes from the field and then methodically cashing in on his numerous foul shots. As they say, "He made his living at the line." When he retired in 1991, only eight NBA stars had scored more career points than Dantley.

One player from long ago, York Larese, never had a problem with the 10-second free throw time limit—it was his habit to shoot his free throws very quickly. On one occasion, referee Mendy Rudolph gave Larese the ball, and the seemingly jittery player shot it so fast that Rudolph couldn't avoid the ball, and, as Gary M. Pomerantz wrote in his fine book, *Wilt, 1962,* "Larese's free throw skimmed off the top of his head." When Rudolph grumbled to him about the misfire, Larese was genuinely apologetic, saying, "That's just the way I shoot."

He was not alone in having a quirk while at the line. Hal Greer, a member of the 20,000 point club as well as the Hall of Fame, used to shoot jumpers for his foul shots, saying that when he shot them, he was practicing his outside shot, and when he shot his jumpers from the field, he was, in a way, practicing/improving his free throw shooting.

Just a few of the many other men with unusual rituals from the foul line include: Steve Nash, Richard Hamilton, Patrick Ewing, Gilbert Arenas, Paul Pierce, and Jeff Hornacek.

(8) Faking a shot to induce an opponent to jump into the lane too soon for a possible rebound is considered to be a lane violation, but a slight hesitation before taking a shot is probably not going to cause the refs to tweet their

whistles. The penalty for faking a foul shot is simple—the shot, if good, would not count, and, shot good or missed, the other team is awarded the ball. In other words, the attempt would immediately be whistled dead.

It seems to be the case that if a player has a hitch in his free throw shot, it is much like a pitcher's unorthodox move prior to making a pitch (think of a gyrating Luis Tiant or Tim Lincecum) with umpires tending to refuse to make a balk call. They would say, "It's his natural movement and he's not trying to deceive the batter. Plus batters know that's just his style." Likewise, none of several longtime observers of basketball could remember established players who possessed a slight hesitation in their free throws ever getting called for such a slight idiosyncrasy.

Then there's Anthony Mason. An excellent website, Bleacher Report (bleacherreport.com), said his foul shots "had so much hesitation you might have thought Will Smith could've starred in a lame romantic comedy about it (i.e., *Hitch*)." His antics, the website reported, actually drew many violations from opponents who were lured into the lane prematurely. Bleacher Report also conjured up the name of Karl Malone as another player with many free throw rituals and a hitch in his shot at the free throw line, as well.

9 This question is a tricky one in that the answer is this: Under the rules, Smith could do absolutely nothing. What he did do, however, was bluff. An account of this odd set of circumstances from the book *Wilt, 1962* has Smith telling Ruklick that he was attempting "to influence the outcome of a regularly scheduled game." He further threatened to forfeit the game to New York, strip the scoring record from Chamberlain, and make sure that Ruklick was banned from the NBA for life. A fearful Ruklick wound up missing both shots, apparently in an unsuspicious manner, and no action was taken against him. The Knicks got the rebound, and the game concluded with a score of 147 for the Knicks and 169 for the Philadelphia Warriors. Chamberlain accounted for almost 60 percent of his team's scoring output.

(10) Ruklick's situation was a bit different, especially because he vocalized what he was about to do and because he didn't follow through on his scheme. A player may intentionally miss a free throw, as refs aren't mind readers, but in order to avoid committing a violation on such a play, his shot must hit or at the very least scrape some rim. Hitting only the backboard or net, or coming up empty with an air ball on a foul shot, results in the loss of possession.

(11) Chamberlain normally would have been given two shots here. However, in the bonus situation, a player had "three to make two." If he sank his first two attempts, then play would continue; if he didn't make his first two, then he was given a third try. In this case, he did underhand his first shot through the net, missed on his second try, and then connected on the bonus to

give him his 92nd point at the 2:28 mark in the final quarter.

At one time in the NBA, the penalty for committing a foul in the backcourt was two shots with the provision of giving "three to make two" if the guilty party was over the foul limit.

Taking a timeout from the answers for a moment, here are some related anecdotes about free throw shooting, Chamberlain and his prowess, and a little more trivia tossed in.

In a 1974 NBA game, Elmore Smith, who was a notoriously poor free throw shooter (like Chamberlain), was in the three-to-make-two situation because of a then-existing rule (the other team had committed more than four team fouls in a quarter, and Smith had been hacked in the act of shooting). Amazingly, Smith proceeded to miss all three shots—and miss them badly. He came up with three straight air balls. Not at all surprisingly, he ended the season as the worst free throw shooter in the league at .485. That same season, he hit on .493 of his shots from the field, meaning, as one source pointed out, "that he made a higher percentage of his shots when someone guarded him."

Of course, when Chris Dudley entered the ranks of the NBA, he soon made everyone cringe when he went to the line. He shot a woeful .458 lifetime with a season-worst .305 from the line (32-of-105 in 1989–1990) versus his best percentage ever, a mere .563 (40 for 71). In one game, the 6' 11" Cleveland Cavalier backup center was fouled in the act of shooting and promptly missed both of his foul shots. On the second attempt, Washington's Darrell Walker entered the lane prematurely, so Dudley was given another shot; he misfired. This time, Dave Feitl of the Bullets committed a lane violation. On the ensuing shot, which Dudley missed, Feitl again entered into the lane early. Given what was in effect a *five-to-make-one* opportunity, Dudley cemented his reputation as a lousy free throw shooter, reportedly becoming the first NBA player ever to go 0-for-5 in one "session" at the line.

Still later came Ben Wallace with his painful lifetime free throw percentage of .414 and his personal season high of .490 (meaning he *never* managed to hit on half his foul shots for a full season—through 2011–2012). He convinced many experts that they had finally witnessed the worst player at the line ever.

As for Rick Barry and his shooting skills, well, he is the only player ever to lead the NCAA, where he starred for the University of Miami (Florida), and the NBA in scoring and was the career scoring leader in the ABA. Barry led the nation in scoring for Miami in 1965, topped the NBA in 1966–1967, and topped all ABA players with a lifetime mark of 30.5 ppg. Counting ABA play, Barry led his league in free throw accuracy seven times over his 14-year pro career, and that included being the best foul shooter around in six of his final eight seasons.

By the way, 40 years after Chamberlain put up his 100-point game, only four NBA *teams* could muster an average of that many points per game, and during the season he hit for those 100 markers in that memorable game (which helped him reach 4,000 points, a total more than 1,000 points higher than any other NBA player had ever reached), only six other players in the league averaged 27 ppg. Interestingly enough, Chamberlain's 100 tallies demolished the old record (which he had set earlier) by 27 points. Not only that, but according to nba.com, Chamberlain pounded down 59 points in the second half of the game in which he hit the century mark, and only 23 other players in the NBA have ever scored more than that total in entire contests.

Chamberlain was no stranger to 50-plus-point outings. His first 50-point game in the NBA came in his eighth game in the league, and, going into his historic contest, he was coming off games in which he had scored 67, 65, and 61 points, respectively. He was truly a one-man wrecking crew, as he had always been. As a high school senior, he averaged more than 45 ppg. and once scored 90 points for Overbrook High even though each quarter in high school games is only eight minutes long versus 12 in the NBA. Prorated, his 90 points works out to an unfathomable 135 points over a 48-minute contest.

Need extra evidence of his utter domination? Over his illustrious career, Michael Jordan hit the 50-point plateau 31 times in regular season play, second best to Chamberlain, who reached that level 118 times including a shocking 30 times in one season—that's 20 times more than the second-best player of all time for a given season (Kobe Bryant). In a seven-game stretch back in 1961, Chamberlain hit for 50 or more points on each of those seven occasions he suited up. That same season, he also strung together streaks of six games and five games (twice) with 50+ points. For that stellar year, he *averaged* 50.4 ppg., which represents the most productive single season output of all time. By way of comparison, the next-best season averages are 44.8, 38.4, and 37.6, all by Chamberlain, giving him the top four scoring seasons ever (and five of the best six). Furthermore, the 65+ level for points scored in a game has been reached just 22 times in the annals of the game, with Chamberlain being responsible for 15 of those binges. If you up the ante to 70 or more points in a single contest, Chamberlain was the "explorer," six of the 10 times that stratum was attained.

The Dipper, who averaged 30.07 ppg. for his career, which is second only to Jordan's 30.12, even posted a game in which he yanked down a record 55 rebounds against Bill Russell and averaged an ungodly 22.9 rebounds per game over his entire career with an NBA season record of 27.2 recorded in 1960–61, to boot. Not to diminish his talents, but it is noteworthy that when he broke into the league, there were just four players who were taller than 6′ 9″ according to author Mark Heisler. Of course, he was still around the league when other giants such as Kareem Abdul-Jabbar broke into the pro ranks.

Chamberlain could do it all. Not content to simply lead the league repeatedly in scoring (seven times), field goal percentage (nine times), and rebounding (11 times over his 13 full seasons), Chamberlain became the only center ever to lead the league in assists. In the 1972–1973 season, he set another NBA record when he sank field goals at a .727 clip, the highest percentage in the history of the league; and, by way of contrast, the ABA's best ever was a mere .604. The only other time a player flirted with the .700 mark for shooting percentage was during the 1966–1967 season, when Chamberlain hit on .683 of his action shots. That season also saw him enjoy a blistering stretch in which he made 35 consecutive shots over a four-game period. As of 2017–2018, the only person to come close to this astonishing feat has been DeAndre Jordan, who had a .714 field goal percentage during the 2016–2017 season.

Unbelievable!

Chamberlain's strength and durability are legendary: during the 1961–62 season, Wilt averaged 48.52 minutes per game, an eye-popping statistic, as NBA games are only 48 minutes long! Due to his being involved in 10 overtime periods, he actually managed to amass 3,882 minutes played over that tremendous season, being on the court from opening buzzer to game's conclusion on 79 of his team's 80 contests, including a triple-overtime affair. Furthermore, he only missed action one time all year long, when with eight minutes to play in a game, he was ejected from the contest. Over his career, the tireless tower of a man averaged 45.8 minutes per game, resting rarely and only briefly.

It should be noted that there have been other stunning point outputs at levels lower than the NBA. Frank Selvy once scored an incredible 100 points in a single game (hitting on 41-of-66 field goals with 18 free throws made), while at Furman against Newberry College. His February 13, 1954, 100-point game is the only time a player ever reached the century plateau, as recognized by the NCAA, at the Division I level, and he was only able to hit that mark when his shot from 40 feet capped off his scoring frenzy at the final buzzer in a 149–95 rout. That game—along with many other stellar ones—helped him establish an NCAA record (since broken numerous times) of 2,538 career points. In 1953–1954, he not only chalked up his 100-point game, but also hit for 50 or more tallies on eight occasions and averaged a sterling 41.7 ppg. He was the first college player to churn out 1,000 points in a single season.

Neither Selvy's nor Chamberlain's 100-point scoring spree stands as the all-time record for a single basketball contest. Clarence "Bevo" Francis played for a small Ohio school named Rio Grande College—so small that even when they excelled, they didn't play any home games in their gym (as it could hold just 200 spectators). In the 1952–1953 season, his team certainly did excel as they rambled to a 39–0 slate including the January 9, 1953, victory in which Francis scored an astonishing 116 points when Rio Grande cruised to a 150–85 decision over Ashland [Kentucky]. If that output isn't impressive enough, get this: in the final 10 minutes of the game, he blazed in 55 points. Coincidentally, his new record broke the former mark of 87, also set by a Rio Grande player (Jack Duncan, 1940–1941).

The 6' 9" Francis later stated, "By the third shot, I knew I was on to something special." Still, he said he didn't realize he had scored as many points as he had until he emerged from the shower and was informed that he had clicked on 47 field goals and 22 free throws. He added that his Ashland opponents "tried everything to stop me. They were pushing. They were shoving. They even put three men on me." He further stated that an examination of his shooting chart, done many years later, revealed that had he played in the era of the three-point shot, he would have scored 164 points.

However, because he achieved his 116-point scoring splurge that night against a two-year college—a national coaches association stripped him of this record two months later—neither the NAIA nor the NCAA recognized his feat. Duncan's old record was also stricken from the books.

The following season against a school that did take part in a four-year program, Francis, who compiled a career average of 48.9 ppg., again shattered the 100-point mark, and this time, on Groundhog's Day, his 113-point explosion on 38 for 70 shooting from the field and 37-of-42 from the line versus Hillsdale College (Michigan) did count. It still stands as a single-game record. His total field goals and free throws made also set records. Francis also hit for 84 and 82 points in other 1954 contests and he outscored the entire opposition in nine college contests. He was a veritable scoring machine.

There have been very few 100-point collegiate games officially recognized by the NCAA. Selvy and Francis did this yet never played a single minute in the NBA.

As of this writing, the 100-point level has been reached 28 times internationally, 19 times in men's high school play, and, counting all games regardless of whether it was at the DI level or not, six times on the collegiate level—twice by Francis, once by Paul Arizin (versus a junior college), once by Selvy, and two times by the most recent player to do this, Jack Taylor of Grinnell College. In fact, Taylor's 138 markers in November of 2012 versus Faith Baptist in a 179-104 victory is the all-time high at the college level.

One quick example of dynamic scoring from the high school level also took place in the prolific 1953–1954 era. Dick Bogenrife, a sixteen-year-old junior at Midway High School set the Ohio scholastic scoring record on February 6, 1953, with 120 points (hitting on 52-of-64 field goal attempts, many coming on cheap cherry-picking opportunities, and 16-of-20 foul shots) in a 32-minute contest. His school, which would graduate just five boys and eight girls in his class, pounded another tiny school, Canaan, by a score of 137–46 behind Bogenrife, their 6′ 2″ center. He would wind up playing, but not racking up much playing time, for the Dayton Flyers from 1955 to 1958.

Incidentally, after running up the score on Canaan,

Midway would get trounced the very next night by Tecumseh High, 107–55. Future NBA star Wayne Embry, then already standing 6' 7", led Tecumseh High with 25 points while holding Bogenrife to exactly 100 fewer points than he had scored on his historic night.

Only twice has a high schooler scored more than Bogenrife did in his record-setting contest. One is Danny Heater, who is said to own the world's high school record with his 135-point performance during a regulation game held on January 26, 1960. He hit for 85 in the second half with 55 of those points coming in the final 10 minutes of the game and pulled down 32 rebounds as well for his Burns-ville (West Virginia) squad, leading the team to a 173–43 annihilation. On that night, he shot 53-of-70 from the field. He could have had even more points but missed 12 of his 41 free throws. The other person to have bested Bogenrife in this category is John Morris from Virginia, with 127 points.

More than a few women have hit for 100, too, including big names like Lisa Leslie and the sister of NBA star Reggie Miller, Cheryl Miller, who would later coach, of all people, Lisa Leslie at the University of Southern California (USC). In Leslie's case, all of her 101 points came in the game's *first half!* At the end of that half, her Morningside, California, team led 102–24, so a scoring summary showed just two people's names for Morningside. At that point, their opponents forfeited the game.

Finally, as recently as 2013, another player hit the 100-point stratum. That took place when Clark Quijano of the Philippines poured in 120 points during a contest.

Whew! Enough asides, back to the answers.

(12) There would have been no call back then, because the 24-second clock was not put into use until the following season. When fans and the league became disgusted with stalling tactics aimed at men such as George Mikan, the need for a shot clock became so apparent that the league added the time limit rule regarding attempting a field goal for the 1954–1955 season.

In one Pistons-Lakers contest held on November 22, 1950, Fort Wayne players froze the ball, and Minneapolis refused to come out of their zone to attack the ball handlers. The result was an 8–7 score at the conclusion of the first quarter, a 13–11 halftime score, and a 17–16 score by the end of the third quarter. Unbelievably (especially to modern fans), only four total points were tallied in the final stanza, and the Pistons won an embarrassing 19–18 game on a shot with just nine seconds to go. That bucket mercifully clinched the lowest-scoring game in NBA history. Mikan shot 11 times and was responsible for 15 of his team's 18 points, and he sank the only four field goals made by the Lakers. A headline in the *Minneapolis Tribune* the next morning read: "LAKERS DEFEATED 19–18; THAT'S CORRECT, 19–18."

A 1954 playoff game actually featured more foul shots attempted than field goals scored, with seventy-five free throws attempted and just thirty-four baskets made.

In a January 1951 contest, the longest game in NBA history took place, languishing on for six overtime sessions. It lasted so long primarily due to Rochester's strategy of sitting on the ball in O.T. versus Indianapolis. Tied at 63 at the end of regulation, the game ended in a 75–73 win after 78 lethargic minutes. In the 30 minutes of overtime play, just 23 shots were attempted. The game ended with the final quarter's only points coming on a layup with one second left on the clock. Such blemishes on the game led to the use of the shot clock.

After all, who wanted to watch a sport that was full of ennui, with infrequent attempts to put points on the board? As Bob Cousy once put it, "That was the way the game was played—get a lead and put the ball in the icebox."

The shot clock innovation yielded instant results. Teams averaged 13.6 points per game more than they had the previous season, and the Boston Celtics became the first NBA squad ever to average more than 100 points per game for a full season. Three years later, each and every NBA team, on average, hit for 100+ points nightly.

Another rule came along the same year the shot clock revolutionized the game. In fact, hoopedia.nba .com states that the two rules went hand in hand, with each one making the other one work. The clock made it "unnecessary for the trailing team to foul deliberately" if they could just play defense for 24 (or fewer) seconds, then hopefully get the ball back on, say, a defensive rebound or a turnover. The other rule, which gave a penalty foul shot after a team committed a sixth foul in a given quarter, "made it too costly to foul to prevent a chance at a basket."

(13) Yes, zones were permitted, but the league quickly outlawed them, doing so on January 11, 1947.

Since then, other changes were made to the rules regarding zones. For example, before the 1966–1967 season, some "language" regarding the Zone Defense rule was added, stating that a defender was not permitted to "station himself in the key area longer than three seconds if it is apparent he is making no effort to play an opponent." This rule applied once the team with the ball advanced it into its frontcourt, and the three-second count began when the offensive team was "in clear control in the front court."

A slew of rules dealing with zone defenses came about in time for the 1981–1982 season and included items such as mandating a defender to "come to a position above foul line" when an offensive player was also above the top of the circle. The rule also noted that after a team was guilty of an illegal defense, the shot clock would be reset to 24 seconds, but beyond that first infraction, a team playing an illegal defense was punished by having the other team shoot a free throw and then keeping possession of the ball.

(14) According to Hoopedia (hoopedia.com), even way back in 1946, the rules gave a player six personal fouls before he fouled out of a game. However, the website also states

that after a while, still early on in NBA history, it took just five personal fouls for a player to become disqualified.

On January 15, 1982, Scott Lloyd of the Dallas Mavericks became the first player to ever suffer the ignominy of fouling out of a pro basketball game while collecting six personal fouls in a single quarter. Lloyd was no stranger to fouling—although he played just 14 minutes per game that season, he fouled out of six games.

Then there was Dick Farley, a Syracuse guard, whom author Norm Hitzges reported to have fouled out of a game against the St. Louis Hawks on March 12, 1956, in just five minutes of play. Normally, though, Farley stayed out of foul trouble—that entire season he would only foul out one more time, and through his first two seasons, covering 141 games, he fouled out a grand total of three times.

(15) True. This strange rule really existed a long time ago when the league was tinkering with rules, groping for solutions such as this attempt to curtail intentional fouling and rough play.

A similar rule that had a slight variation came along two seasons later when rule makers spotted a flaw in their earlier rule—at times, coaches purposely had tall players foul shorter men, giving them an edge on the ensuing jump balls. The new rule stated that the jump ball would take place between the man who had just been fouled and "the player who is guarding him."

16 This one is also true but was done away with once rule makers saw that it was not preventing teams from fouling late in contests.

17 The distance has been changed over the years, but it currently stands at its original (1980–1981) distance of 23′ 9″ (except for the corners, where the line is 22′ away from the middle of the basket). From 1994–1995 through 1996–1997, the distance was cut to 22′ across the board, but that lasted only until 1997–1998.

18 The ball was red, white, and blue.

19 True. By the same token, if even one millimeter of a player's foot is on the three-point line when he lets the ball fly on a field goal attempt, that shot can only count for two points because he's considered to now be out of three-point territory.

20 The third ref was added to the NBA in 1988. "Two officials," noted veteran NBA and ABA ref Ed T. Rush, "have very little chance of consistently legislating contact off the ball. With the type of athlete you have today, the strength, size, speed, you just have to have that extra pair of eyes."

21 NBA courts are 94 feet long and 50 feet wide.

(22) Although it was believed to be an NBA first, Barry's request was granted. One Houston front office worker said it reminded him of the days when high school and college players wore even numbers at home and odd-numbered jerseys as visitors.

(23) Common sense, and the rules of the NBA, say this strategy is illegal.

(24) This is basically the same issue as the previous question—it is also illegal.

(25) Wave off the bucket—better yet, don't call it a basket in the first place. The rule forbidding the ball from entering the basket from below began before the 1977–1978 season.

(26) No, he has run out of time. This is a three-second lane violation. While a player is permitted to be in the lane, leave it, then reenter it to start the three-second count again, and do such moves indefinitely, on this play, Maravich, under basketball rules, never left the paint. Here is how the rulebook reads on this matter: "A player shall not remain for more than three seconds in that part of his free throw lane between the endline and extended 4' (imaginary) off the court and the edge of the free throw line while the ball is in control of his team."

Strictly speaking, if a player whose team had control of the ball took a spill, landed in the imaginary extended area mentioned above, and found that an injury had left him nearly immobile, the rules extend no mercy to him. He would still have only three seconds to roll, crawl, hobble, or, if he had the ability, levitate out of there before he would be guilty of a three-second violation.

Mark Pena, a veteran official, mainly referring to high school and college play, explained that there is "kind of a fallacy on how three seconds [calls] work. The rule says that if you're in the lane for three seconds, it's a violation; but, if I pass you the ball and you're in the key and you held it for 2 or 2 1/2 seconds and then you made a move to the basket, we would allow you to continue the move. Now, if you stop the move and picked up your dribble without shooting, then we would call the three seconds." Likewise, says Pena, most refs would, in this question, probably allow a fallen player to get up and out of the lane area rather than whistle him for three seconds.

As for Pete Maravich, well . . . he was a consummate showman on the court, armed with a repertoire of skills that included stunning no-look passes from everywhere—behind the back, between the legs, etc.—and the dribbling prowess of Harlem Globetrotter caliber.

He was coached by his dad, Petar "Press" Maravich, at LSU, a team that went 3–23 during Press's first season as the head coach, the year Pete was a freshman back when the rules declared a freshman could not play varsity ball. Despite Pete's many talents, the next two seasons LSU would improve, but only to a level around .500—posting a 14–12, then a 13–13 slate. By the time Pete was a senior, the team went 21–10.

Pete was only the second sophomore to lead the nation in scoring; Oscar Robertson had been the first. The 1970 Player of the Year dazzled fans with 28 games in which he pounded down 50 or more points, good for one of many Maravich records.

His exact scoring outputs were as superbly consistent as they were awesome: 43.8 as a sophomore, a new NCAA record; 44.2 in his junior year, smashing his own record; and 44.5 as a senior, obviously yet another record. Even his worst output of those three seasons produced an average of 2.1 ppg. higher than the #4 man on the list, Frank Selvy. It follows that he topped the NCAA in scoring for three years running, copping All-American honors in each of those seasons.

After scoring 50 or more points nine times in his first two seasons at LSU, he set a record by connecting for 50+ ten times as a senior. His point totals of 1,148 as a junior and 1,381 as a senior were both all-time highs. By the time he unlaced his sneakers for the last time at LSU, he had amassed a jaw-dropping 3,667 points, good for an all-time high of 44.2 ppg., passing Oscar Robertson by an impressive 694 points as the top scorer ever in NCAA play.

On February 25, 1977, the "Pistol" was on fire, tickling the nets for 68 points. It was a new NBA record for a guard, and his point total let him attain a level that had been reached before by just two men: Wilt Chamberlain and Elgin Baylor. That same season, Maravich became just the fourth guard in NBA history to average over 30 ppg. In fact, in the 1970s, the kid out of LSU trailed just three NBA stars for total points.

In 1996, his body of work was recognized when he was selected as a member of the 50 Greatest Players in NBA History (which was decided in 1996).

(27) Yes, an NBA team may make a protest. Here's an example of a game that had to be replayed from the point of a protest. On March 23, 1979, the Philadelphia 76ers met the New Jersey Nets to conclude a protested game from the previous November, one that the Sixers had won. The Nets protested that contest, saying the refs had hit coach Kevin Loughery and forward Bernard King with three technical fouls each, violating the rule limiting techs to two per game. The NBA agreed with the Nets' contention and instructed the teams to play the final 17:50 of the game. The protest turned out to be pointless in that Philadelphia again emerged as the victors.

An oddity here is that during the several months between the games, the Nets and Sixers had made a trade involving four players. All of them had played in the original game. Technically speaking, these four men wound up playing for both the winning and losing teams of the same game.

(28) The defensive player must either be guarding the man with the ball or he must be "actively guarding any

opponent," which means he has to be "within an arms [*sic*] length of an opponent." The rule further indicates that if a player on offense should pass "through the key, the defender must be within arms [*sic*] length, and also move along with the offensive player." He cannot simply stand nearby "and put his arms out to get a new three second count."

(29) Yes. Everything in this item was correct. Here is how one website defines and explains the difference between goaltending and basket interference and what is legal and what's not when it comes to touching the ball or basket, which is considered to be the "basket ring, the flange, braces, and the net" (while also realizing the backboard is not considered to be a part of the basket). Goaltending occurs when a player "touches the ball during a tip, bat or try for field goal while the ball is entirely above the basket on its downward flight, is not in the imaginary cylinder, and has the possibility of entering the basket."

As for basket interference, it is the "illegal touching of the ball when it is in the cylinder, on the ring, within the basket, regardless of how the ball got there. Touching the basket when the ball is on or within the basket is always classified as basket interference." Similarly, the same applies when a player reaches "through the basket from below" and touches the basketball before it goes into the cylinder. However, it is not basket interference to touch the basket while the ball is in the imaginary cylinder above the ring level.

There can be defensive and offensive goaltending or basket interference calls, and if the ball is on the rim and a player touches the net, this is also basket interference. Furthermore, there are even a few more specifics regarding these violations, but the above should suffice here.

(30) True. The rules also state that a defender who is inside the lower defensive box may also use an extended forearm and do so any time he wishes in order "to maintain his position against a player with the ball." However, he may never use the forearm "to dislodge, reroute or impede the offensive player."

(31) This hand-checking item is true. The rulebook also, according to nba.com, states that a player on the defensive squad "may not place and keep his hand on an opponent unless he is in the area near the basket and the offensive player has his back to the basket."

(32) According to an article in *The Plain Dealer,* in such cases the rule, sometimes called the "Wilt Chamberlain Rule," declares that if a player is fouled before the ball is inbounded or when the foul takes place away from the ball in the last two minutes of the game, free throws are awarded to the player, *and* his team also retains the ball.

Likewise, under the same time frame mentioned in this question, the same penalty is doled out if a defender "takes a foul against an offensive player who is not part of the action." The rule was drawn up to prevent teams from employing the strategy of fouling poor free throw shooters "to gain an advantage in the critical part of a game."

(33) A flagrant foul gives two foul shots to the team that was fouled, and they maintain possession of the basketball. The more serious flagrant foul 2 also leads to the player who committed the foul being ejected after the play was reviewed using instant replay. In addition, any player who is guilty of committing two flagrant foul 1s in the same game is ejected.

The league takes into consideration other factors when they review flagrant fouls to determine if a player is to, for example, be fined and/or suspended. Among other items they scrutinize are how severe the contact was, how severe an injury to the player who was fouled may have been, whether "the fouling player wound up and/or followed through after making contact" with his arm or hand, and "the outcome of the contact (e.g., whether it led to an altercation)."

(34) True. Such contact is known as incidental or marginal contact. For instance, the rules indicate that players are permitted "normal body contact with opponents when reaching for a loose ball if they both have the same opportunity to get the ball." Such contact is incidental when neither man is illegally gaining an advantage. Likewise, the rules state that a player's hand is, as the old saying goes, "part of the ball" when it is making contact

NBA REFEREES:
(FROM LEFT TO RIGHT)
TOM WASHINGTON,
MONTY MCCUTCHEN,
AND BRENT BARNAKY

with the basketball. Thus, no call is made on a defender who "makes normal contact" on a player's hand when it is making contact with the ball.

(35) Yes, the quote from this question was taken directly from nba.com. Another website, ihoops.com, added this related item: "One of the basic tenets [regarding traveling] is that a player cannot travel unless that player is holding a live ball. A bobble or fumble is not 'control' of the ball, therefore, it cannot be a traveling violation."

(36) The website nba.com provides definitions to clarify this question. Illegal picks or screens occur when a player from the team with the ball is not in a legal position. That is to say, he disobeys such conditions as these: "When picking a stationary opponent from the backside, you must give that player a step. When picking a stationary opponent from the front or side, a player can go right next to him as long as he does not make illegal contact. If the opponent is moving, you must get to your position and give him an opportunity to stop and/or change direction. The speed of the player will determine the distance. You cannot just jump in front of a moving opponent at the last second."

We'll trust you to grade yourself on this one—if you feel you expressed the basics of these rules, take credit for this question.

(37) This is yet again what nba.com sees as a rule misunderstood by many fans. Many refs consider the block vs.

charging decision to be the toughest one to make on the court. These fouls take place when a defender attempts "to get in front of his man to stop him from going in that direction." If he doesn't get into the proper position before contact occurs, the refs must call a blocking foul on the defender because he didn't give, say, the man with the ball a chance to avoid the contact. However, if the defender has established a legal position and the contact is the fault of the player from the offensive team, it's a charging foul. Plus, if there should be marginal contact, "no foul may be called."

Let's get more precise. In order for a player to get into what's considered a legal position, in which he is "defending against the dribble, the defender needs to get his torso directly in the path and beat him to the spot. On a drive to the basket, the defender must get his position before the shooter starts his upward shooting motion. For off ball players, the defender must get into position and allow enough opportunity for the offensive player to stop and/or change direction. All ties are considered blocks as the defender did not beat him to the spot but arrived at the same time."

The website ihoops.com also states that contrary to what most fans believe, a defensive player does not have to be stationary in order to take a charge. The site elaborates, "Once a defensive player has obtained a legal guarding position, the defensive player may always move to maintain that guarding position and may even have one or both feet off the floor when contact occurs with the offensive player." The site defines a legal guarding position as one in which the man guarding the dribbler has both feet on the floor while also is in the position of facing the dribbler.

(38) It's difficult to fathom Robertson dribbling out of control, but even if he did, as ihoops.com explains, "There is no restriction as to how high a player may bounce the ball, provided the ball does not come to rest in the player's hand."

Trying to stop Robertson was as impossible as winning a wager on the Washington Generals to upset the Harlem Globetrotters (although, as a noteworthy aside, it's a fact that in their early years, the 'Trotters did, on occasion, lose—in the winter of 1927, they lost 16 of their 117 contests; then again, by 1948, they defeated the Lakers of George Mikan in an exhibition game).

Robertson's brilliance was evident early on. For example, in college, he became the first sophomore to ever lead the nation in scoring, doing so in 1957–1958 with 35.1 ppg. When he left the campus of the University of Cincinnati, he ranked number one on the all-time NCAA scoring list.

Of course, he played in the era when there was a rule that prohibited freshman from playing on the varsity level, which deprived fans of an extra year of witnessing the sparkling skills of the Big O. Still, this legendary Hall of Fame guard quickly went on to become an elite NBA player (he led the league in assists in five of his first seven seasons), one who made the list of the 50 Greatest Players in NBA History, averaging 7.5 rebounds, 9.5 assists (#4 in NBA history), and 25.7 points (ninth best all-time in NBA play) each time he took to the court. With those astonishing numbers, one of his most amazing feats was when he averaged a triple-double for an entire season (1961–1962), a feat only accomplished by one other NBA player (Russell Westbrook, who did it twice).

(39) You can give yourself partial credit if you guessed 10 seconds, because that's what the rule had been for some time. However, before the start of the 1976–1977 season, the NBA rule makers changed it, giving teams in situations such as these "the unexpired time [on the shot clock] or 5 seconds, whichever is longer, to attempt a shot." Anytime the team with the ball was entitled to a throw-in and the shot clock read less than 5 seconds, the officials were to reset that clock to 5 seconds.

(40) 30 seconds.

(41) True, although $25 even in those days was probably not much of a deterrent to a showboating player.

(42) Although this may sound odd, it's true—a player who, for example, grabbed a rebound off a missed free throw had to come down and make contact with the floor before he was permitted to try to score.

(43) The team could pass the ball in from either "midcourt or at the out of bounds spot."

(44) The correct answer, and the most logical one, is "B," the opposing coach makes the call.

(45) The rule here states the basket is to be disallowed. Here are a handful of interesting plays involving that rule. In March 2003, Ricky Davis, with a selfish motive in mind, purposely shot at the wrong basket—well, almost. Needing one rebound to reach a triple-double, the Cavs guard had possession of the ball after Utah's Scott Padgett scored with 6 seconds to play in the game. Davis was prepared to shoot at the wrong basket so he would be able to get his own rebound in order to complete the triple-double. Utah's DeShawn Stevenson "wrapped his arms around Davis before the attempt and was whistled for the foul." Jazz coach Jerry Sloan observed, "Let him try to get it when the game means something. I was proud of DeShawn, and I would have knocked him down harder."

In the 2009–2010 season, Nate Robinson of the Knicks made his coach and many fans angry when he took an inbounds pass not too far from the New Jersey bucket with 0.5 seconds left in the first quarter. Instead of heaving a long shot or simply sitting on the ball to kill the time left in that period, he turned around and shot at the Nets basket—and sank the shot. Luckily, the clock had just expired before he got the shot off, but had time not run out, it seems as if, by rule, the bucket, certainly shot intentionally by Robinson, would have counted for New Jersey, and because of the distance of his shot, it would have placed three points on the board for the Nets.

Another tale has Chris Mills of Golden State shooting at the Dallas Mavs basket after securing a jump ball in a 1999 contest. Samaki Walker of the Mavericks must have been confused, too, because he blocked the Mills layup! Dennis G. Schmuck posted an article on the Internet about the play, wondering such interesting thoughts as would the basket have counted had it gone in, given that the shot was taken intentionally, and should goaltending have come into play on the call.

According to one website, a nonshooting foul was called on Walker, and the Warriors got to inbound the ball to resume play. It was also reported that initially Golden State's Coach P.J. Carlesimo argued that Mills should have been allowed to shoot two free throws, but the refs countered by saying, in effect, "Fine, but he'll have to shoot at the Dallas basket."

NCAA MEN'S RULES AND SITUATIONS

Let's start this chapter out with a rather odd question, and it's a good guess here that if you get this one correct, it was just exactly that—a good *guess* on your part, because this rule dates back quite some time. Plus, the answer to this one is peculiar. For that matter, so are all of the possible answers.

Here's one rule that doesn't pertain to men's rules, but a variation of those rules.

(1) Just one year after Dr. Naismith introduced the game of basketball, a physical education teacher at Smith College in Massachusetts named Senda Berenson tailored the rules to make them more suitable for women. Now imagine you were watching a women's game back then, and take a stab at this question. Berenson's rules included making it illegal for a player to:

    A) dribble the ball more than seven times before making a pass or handing the ball off to a teammate

    B) steal the ball

    C) make substitutions unless a player was injured

    D) all three of the above items

Answer on page 87

We'll consider the next several items as college questions, ones that deal with Dr. Naismith's original 13 rules for the game.

(2) Each of the following multiple choices lists one of those rules except one—pick that one to get credit for this question.

> A) The basketball "may be thrown in any direction using one or both hands."
> B) "The ball may be batted in any direction with one or both hands, but never with the fist."
> C) "A player cannot run with the ball. The player must throw it from the spot on which he catches it, allowance to be made for a man running at a good speed."
> D) "A player on the team which possesses the ball may never touch the basket."

Answer on page 87

(3) Which of the following was not one of Naismith's original 13 rules?

> A) "If any side persists in delaying the game, the umpire shall call a foul on them."
> B) "When a ball goes out of bounds, it shall be thrown into the field and played by the first person touching it. In case of dispute the umpire shall throw it straight into the field."

C) "A goal shall be made when the ball is thrown or batted from the grounds into the basket and stays there, providing those defending the goal do not touch or disturb the goal. If the ball rests on the edges, and the opponent moves the basket, it shall count as a goal."

D) "If either side makes three consecutive fouls it shall count as a goal for the opponents (consecutive means without the opponents in the meantime making a foul)."

E) "If a player holds, pushes, strikes or trips an opponent it shall be declared a foul the first time such an action occurs, but it shall disqualify a player for the duration of the game the second time he does such an action."

Answer on pages 87–89

④ In February 2012, an Alabama freshman named Jack Blankenship became a sort of overnight Internet sensation when he used a huge picture of his face, which for the purposes of creating a distraction, he had contorted wildly. Writer Jeff Eisenbert reported that Blankenship was well aware that students on other campuses had been waving "giant celebrity heads" of people such as "a snarling Saddam Hussein, to a grinning Hulk Hogan, to a sultry Marilyn Monroe" in order to bother opponents at the free throw line. So he decided to try his own approach. When ESPN2 cameras captured his amusing antics that took place

ALABAMA STUDENT
AND FAN, JACK BLANKENSHIP

during Alabama's two-point win in overtime against Mississippi, Blankenship gained fame.

However, the question is this—did his actions to annoy opponents break any NCAA rules, and was he forced to cease and desist?

Answer on pages 89–95

5 When Clemson met Maryland on February 7, 2012, a rather odd play occurred near the end of the game, which left the fans baffled by the officials' call. Maryland was looking for their first win at Clemson in nearly five years, and they were clinging to a 63–62 lead with just 2.8 seconds left to play. Then Maryland guard Sean Mosley hit on one of two free throws, setting up the play in question.

Milton Jennings heaved a pass that traveled almost the length of the court, but it was picked off by Mosley. However, it was ruled that Mosley was out of bounds when he made contact with the basketball. Where did the officials have Clemson inbound the game's final play—where Mosley was when he intercepted the pass, where Jennings was when he released the pass, or somewhere else?

Answer on page 96

6 It was yet another gem in a string of classic matchups between the Duke Blue Devils and the North Carolina Tar Heels on February 8, 2012. Duke hit the road for the short eight-mile trip from their campus to Chapel Hill, North Carolina, and onto the Dean Smith Center— also known

DUKE vs. NORTH CAROLINA

as the Dean Dome—and they fully realized they'd have a battle royal on their hands as the on-the-road underdog. Their rivalry is unquestionably one of the greatest ones in any sport.

Quite fittingly, this one came down to the wire, but only after the Blue Devils clawed back in yet another one of their patented miracle comebacks. Down by as many as 10 points with time dwindling, they would require every one of their points on a 13-to-2 run to pull this one out.

One key play took place with UNC on top, 83–80, at the 20.3 second mark in the game. Roughly three seconds later, Duke's Ryan Kelly, a 6' 11" forward who possesses a nice touch from beyond the three-point line, did in fact put up a shot from long range. He misfired, but the ball was accidentally tipped into the bucket by the Tar Heels' 7' 0" Tyler Zeller, who had leaped very close to the basket for a possible rebound or blocked shot. He first touched the ball, seeming to bat at it, while it was without a doubt outside the hoop's cylinder and definitely on its downward path. Now, is this goaltending or not? If so, some fans wondered, would the refs award Duke three points or two? If it isn't goaltending, then just how would you call this play?

Answer on pages 96–97

(7) Which of the following is considered the official way to determine if time has run out in the half, game, or overtime period:

A) the clock above the basket

B) the buzzer

C) the light on the backboard that goes off as time runs out

D) other

Answer on pages 97–98

(8) Let's say Syracuse star Carmelo Anthony was inbounding the ball back in his glory days with the Orangemen, but his efforts to find a teammate were being thwarted a by full-court press. Worried that he might not be able to get the ball in play under the time limit, he threw the ball to a teammate who had left the court, stepping out of bounds just a few yards from Anthony. A moment later, after Anthony took a step or two onto the court, the teammate inbounded the ball to him. Are they permitted to switch positions like this to get the ball in play?

Answer on page 98

(9) As is the case in the world of professional basketball, some college rules have come about due to the influence and/or impact of one man. One such rule was written to curtail the dominance of Lew Alcindor, and there was no pretense about the reason the rule came about. It even became known informally as the "Lew Alcindor Rule."

Alcindor, who would later change his name to Kareem Abdul-Jabbar and would become the highest-scoring player in NBA history, was a highly touted young man who came out of Power Memorial Academy (a school that also produced Len Elmore, Mario Elie, Chris Mullin, and NBA ref Dick Bavetta) in New York City in 1965. From there, he headed directly to the campus of UCLA. In high school, he once guided his team to a remarkable 71-game winning streak, and his 1964 squad has been called the top high school team of the 20th century. He quickly conquered the college ranks, as well. In 1966–1967, his first season, he was selected as the national player of the year.

In fact, as a member of the freshman team, back when frosh didn't play on the varsity squad, Alcindor's unit frequently beat the tremendous UCLA varsity team when they scrimmaged.

Enough background—here's your easy question: What fan-pleasing offensive weapon was banned in April of 1967, not to be reinstated for nearly 10 years?

Answer on pages 98–102

(10) Long before Alcindor, there was Wilt Chamberlain from the University from Kansas. In his case, his influence on the NCAA rulebook was evident in one rare instance of an action he hadn't even done yet. The fact of the matter is he was responsible for a rule change based solely on what was rumored that he *would do*. Before Chamberlain even donned a Jayhawk uniform, Kansas coach Phog Allen stated that his recruit out of Overbrook High School in Philadelphia would never miss a foul shot. What unusual strategy did he have in mind? The idea Allen had concocted was one that only a superb athlete

could accomplish. Exactly what had Allen and Chamberlain devised?

Answer on pages 102–103

(11) Another rule of note was implemented prior to Chamberlain's college debut. Before him, a player on the team with the ball could stand near the hoop and guide a teammate's shot, redirecting its path through the air and into the hoop . . . but this would become a rules violation. What was this infraction considered—that is, what was the actual call for guiding a shot as described?

Answer on page 103

(12) Switching to Chamberlain's nemesis, the dimensions of one part of the court were changed because of Bill Russell shortly after he led his University of San Francisco Dons to the national title for the 1954–1956 season—what are we referring to here?

Answer on pages 103–105

(13) One of many plays that helped Lehigh send Duke reeling, 75–70, in the NCAA Tournament on March 16, 2012, involved a basic rule of the game. Late in the second half, Lehigh star C.J. McCollum, who wound up with a game-high 30 points, pulled in a long rebound and began to burst out of a pack of players, headed for an apparent breakaway bucket. However, Tyler Thornton reached in for the ball but seemed to also grab McCollum's upper arm, slowing him down. The officials called Thornton for

an intentional foul. What is the punishment for such an act?

Answer on pages 105–106

(14) Earlier there was a question about the NBA shot clock. What about college—how much time is allotted for teams to get off a shot (and, of course, at least hit the rim or enter the basket with that shot)? As a bonus, can you guess within three years when the shot clock came into existence in the college ranks?

Answer on pages 106–107

(15) How much time does a team get to inbound the ball after the other team has scored a field goal?

Answer on page 107

(16) Sometimes a team elects to roll the ball in rather than passing it, usually in an effort to move the ball upcourt before the clock starts in certain circumstances. In such situations, must a player on the offensive team pick the ball up within five seconds after it has been rolled onto the court?

Answer on pages 107–108

(17) According to author Norm Hitzges, this bizarre situation took place in January 1982. The University of California-Santa Cruz was playing West Coast Christian School when, by the 2:10 mark in the second half, every player for W.C.C.S. had fouled out except one. Only 6′ 0″ guard Mike Lockhart remained eligible to play on—but how?

With no one to pass the ball to, what could Lockhart do? Under the rules, did his Knights have to forfeit? Could he inbound the ball to himself, then dribble up court?

Answer on pages 108–109

(18) On March 23, 2012, Ohio University battled #1-seeded UNC to a 63–63 tie at the end of regulation in the Midwest Regional Semifinals of the NCAA Tournament. As the game's first 40 minutes ended, UNC was in the double bonus. Does that carry over into overtime, or do both teams start from scratch as far as bonus situations go?

Answer on page 109

(19) Let's say Michigan State is being pressed by Illinois and the player trying to inbound the ball is struggling to find an open teammate. With his time limit quickly expiring, he simply hands the ball to a fellow Spartan who has cut to a spot just inches away from him. Is this an expedient, safe, and legal strategy?

Answer on page 109

(20) Now let's say the Michigan State player from above spots a teammate who has broken away from the defense and has raced way downcourt. The player inbounding the ball then throws a deep baseball pass that, incredibly, swishes through the net—does this count as a three-pointer?

Answer on page 110

(21) Do refs have the power to terminate a game under certain circumstances, or must all games be played out?

Answer on page 110

(22) Picture a player at the free throw line about to take a shot. An opponent situates himself inside the three-point arc around, say, just a bit to the left of the top of the key. Is this legal or not?

Answer on pages 110–112

(23) What happens when none of the refs get a clear view of which player last touched a ball that went out of bounds?

Answer on pages 112–113

(24) It happens from time to time—as it did in the 2012 National Semifinal game between Kentucky and Louisville—a ball, batted in this case by several players, got wedged between the basket and the backboard. What's the call when this occurs?

Answer on page 113

(25) Speaking of Kentucky, they had to knock off Kansas to win the National Championship in 2012 . . . and they did. One interesting play took place during the early moments of the game when Wildcats guard Doron Lamb drove to the hole for a layup. He got the shot off and was fouled by Travis Releford. In the meantime, while trying to block the shot, Tyshawn Taylor of Kansas had his hand inside the cylinder of the basket from under the rim, apparently

ANTHONY DAVIS

touching both the net and the rim, but not the ball. You make the call.

Answer on pages 113–114

(26) Earlier in the 2012 tournament when Ohio State met Syracuse, Aaron Craft of the Buckeyes bumped into James Southerland near the sideline after he had received an inbounds pass, causing Southerland to lose his balance and fall out of bounds with the basketball. What did the refs call here?

    A) it's a force-out

    B) foul on Craft

    C) in this case, the refs felt the contact was incidental, so a turnover was called

    D) incidental contact, but Syracuse keeps the ball

Answer on page 114

(27) Say Syracuse takes a shot that is batted out of bounds. On the ensuing play, the inbound pass is a deep one, traveling beyond the midcourt line where Rakeem Christmas, wearing jersey number 25 (with a name like that, what other number would he possibly wear?), hauls in the ball. Can he bring the ball back into the frontcourt, or is this an example of over and back?

Answer on page 115

Here's an easy one for older basketball fans, ones who remember the days before the possession arrow became a part of the game:

(28) What occurs when two players battle for the ball and a tie-up occurred—a held ball "stalemate" situation? Would the refs let the players wrestle over the ball until one player emerged with it, or what?

Answer on page 115

(29) Imagine a defensive team has put on a full-court press with nobody guarding the passer but instead employed all five defenders to blanket the other team's remaining four men. In an effort to see the court better and to locate a man to pass the ball in to, may the passer run the baseline under any circumstances during the game? Yes or No?

Answer on page 115

(30) What would you do if you knew a team didn't have any more timeouts, yet a player from that team turns to you and signals for a timeout?

Answer on page 116

(31) An odd play occurred when the Cincinnati Bearcats met the UNC Charlotte 49ers in January 1999. With just under 18 seconds to go, Charlotte went to the free throw line in a one-and-one situation. The Bearcats pulled down the rebound off the first shot, and, second later, Melvin Levett connected on a three-pointer to put his team on top. The refs stepped in and, for some reason—maybe they mistakenly thought they had been in a two-shot foul situation instead of a one-on-one situation—blew the ball dead and took away the three. When refs make

CHRIS WEBBER

a mistake like this, is there something that can be done? What happened in this case?

Answer on page 116

(32) Here's another truly odd one. In a 1952 contest between Drake and Wichita State, a fan, not a player, interfered with the basket. With just a handful of seconds remaining in the tie game, Drake had the ball, working it around for a final shot. When the shot went up, a Wichita State fan sitting in the balcony not far from the Drake bucket threw his coat at the hoop. What do you suppose the refs decided on this play?

Answer on page 116

(33) By current rules, how many teams are invited to participate in the NCAA men's hoop tournament each spring?

Answer on page 117

ANSWERS

(1) The correct answer here is "B." She must have felt permitting players to steal the ball would hamper the game. In addition, Berenson did have a rule making it illegal for a woman to dribble more than *three* times (not seven times, as mentioned in this question). Another rule she drafted, which seems absurd to us today, had the court split into three sections, with each player confined to play in a given area—talk about specialization.

Although the women's game has certainly come a long way, it took quite a bit of time for them to attain a measure of, or at least a semblance of, equality with men. The first NCAA National Championship for women was not held until 1982, when Louisiana Tech won the title against Cheyney State. For the record, it took just four more years for the first women's team to win it all and do so with an unblemished record. Texas accomplished this feat with a spectacular 34–0 mark.

(2) The answer is "D." For some reason, it seems that Naismith was really obsessed with the idea of not having the ball tainted by the fist—he made a separate rule about such an act, declaring it to be a foul to strike "at the ball with the fist."

(3) The rule here that was not among the original 13 was "E," but only because the second infraction as described in this question would not disqualify a player—it would,

87

though, force him out of action, not unlike a penalty in hockey, until the next goal was made. Naismith added a clause to this rule that did provide for a player to sit out the rest of the game if he committed a foul of pushing, striking, etc. As he put it, the disqualification would occur if "there was evident intent to injure the person." Not only that, in such a case, no substitution for that player would be permitted.

(4) There was nothing illegal in the situation with the Crimson Tide fan. If you're curious and want to catch a glimpse of Blankenship's distracting picture, simply search the Internet, and you will quickly gain some insight into what all the fuss was about.

Over the years, fans have come up with a ton of creative ideas to pester free throw shooters, including the twirling of a circular sign that featured the same basic design as the hypnotic ring that used to spin at the start of the old *Twilight Zone.*

Then there was Speedo Guy at Duke. In 2003, Patrick King, wearing only a Speedo, performed a frenetic dance in his unique effort to distract Tar Heel player Jackie Manuel. It worked. Manuel, who later confessed that it had been difficult to concentrate on his task after he had spied Speedo Guy, missed both of his free throws. King wasn't difficult to spot, because, in an orchestrated move, the other fans near him had agreed to sit down when he began his act. A few other fans later followed the original Speedo Guy, imitating the antics of the grad student who went on to become a pastor. Speedo Guy II showed up in 2005, and after he put on his little show, North Carolina's Marvin Williams missed two foul shots.

One NBA fan tried holding up a poster of a bikini model to distract Larry Bird—it had absolutely no effect on the man who would shoot .886 from the free throw line for his career (still twelfth best all-time—Steve Nash at .904 ranks #1 through 2017–2018). Bird also enjoyed a career-high free throw percentage of .930 in the 1989–1990 season. This sensation, who led the league in free throw percentage four times, played 13 seasons in the NBA and was an All-Star a dozen times, missing out on that honor in 1988–1989, when he was injured and played in just six contests. "The Hick from French Lick" (Indiana) became just the third man, and the first one who wasn't a center, to win the Most Valuable Player Award three straight times.

Let's take a timeout to explore some related topics.

Trying to distract the attention of a sharpshooter at the line is like the time (if my memory is correct) that Johnny Carson tried an experiment on *The Tonight Show* with a professional golfer who was asked to demonstrate his putting. What he didn't know was that at just about the time he was to take his shot, Carson had arranged for a scantily clad woman to come out from behind the stage curtains and strut her stuff directly in the putter's line of sight. The trick failed, and the shot was sunk effortlessly.

So just as is the case with baseball and the age-old advice to "keep your eye on the ball," basketball shooters know they must keep their eye on their target, not on *any* type of distraction. It's been said that men such as Price and Micheal Williams, who once set an NBA record by converting 97 straight free throws, could at times in practice hit around 90+ percent of their foul shots while blindfolded. One would think that would also hold true for José Calderón, whose .9805 FT% based on missing just three of his 154 free throws (2008–2009) ranks as the best ever for a season, considerably better than the former record held by Calvin Murphy (.9581) in 1980–1981. As for documentation of uncanny free throw shooting, the *Guinness Book of World Records* states that a man named Fred Newman once made 88 consecutive free throws while blindfolded.

As for the topic of fans' poor behavior during games, if matters get a bit too crazy (going beyond simple distractions), refs do have the power to control the crowd by doing things such as asking security guards to remove a fan or even by stopping a game and threatening to force a forfeit if unruly behavior doesn't cease. Often the coach of the home team will help out, sometimes by grabbing the public address system's microphone to scold, plead, or demand the students to calm down. Finally, while officials can declare a forfeit, such a call is rare and, naturally, made only when all else fails.

The NBA rulebook notes that if a spectator heaps verbal abuse on a player or coach to the point where a game official feels it is interfering with a coach's ability to "communicate with his players during the game and/

or huddles," the crew chief will see to it that the fan is given a warning by a building security officer. If the behavior continues, the crew chief will then have security eject the fan from the game's venue.

On February 18, 2012, in a basketball game played at the college level, it became apparent that it's not just your average obnoxious fan who can get ejected from a game. It turns out that even former collegiate stars are not impervious to the power of referees. When North Carolina State played host to Florida State in Raleigh, North Carolina, two ex-Wolfpack standouts—Tom Gugliotta and Chris Corchiani—found that they were not immune from an ejection. They were watching the game from a spot behind the scorers' table when referee Karl Hess, who felt he had heard enough from them, had them removed from their seats.

Later, the supervisor of officials of the Atlantic Coast Conference, John Clougherty, released a statement saying Rule 10 gives refs the power to request home game management to eject a fan "when the behavior, in the officials' judgment, is extreme or excessive."

Corchiani would later tell CBS Sports that he and Gugliotta contested about seven of Hess's calls and that they "were yelling, but we didn't even yell a profanity or even threaten him. . . . We're not denying we were all over him, but I've been doing that every game I've been at since I retired." Well, not for every full game—Hess had had enough, and the two men were removed with 6:40 left in the North Carolina State defeat.

Mark Pena was working a high school game when he noticed someone in one section of the stands had thrown "something across my face. I ran up and down the court again and I saw another [object] come—it was an M & M. I stopped the game and went over to the security guard and asked him to watch that section." Moments later, another M & M just missed his head, and this time Pena took the matter to the next level, telling the security guy to "clear the entire section—everybody's out of here." Luckily, before those measures had to be taken—measures that Pena didn't really want to enforce—an older fan pointed out the culprit, who was promptly removed. "I got a standing ovation and the game continued. So I do have that ability to do what I did." He added refs could even clear an entire gym if things got ugly—like the time someone used pepper spray at a game he worked: "We got everybody off the court until they cleaned up the mess, got the kids who did it out, then we resumed the game. We could have declared a forfeit if we knew exactly who did it [fans of which team], but that's a last resort."

Back to the issue at hand. By and large, trying to distract a free throw shooter by being as loud as possible is just part of the game. Make no mistake, there have been times in the history of sports when someone went too far in trying to bother an opponent. The New York Giants once had a pesky second baseman named Eddie Stanky, whose actions led to a change in baseball's rulebook after he purposely positioned himself behind the pitcher and directly in the line of vision of an opposing batter. Stanky even began jumping up and down while waving both arms, almost as if he were doing jumping jacks—all to distract the hitter.

This was also seen during the first round of the 2008 Stanley Cup Playoffs between the New York Rangers and the New Jersey Devils. During one of the games, Sean Avery of the Rangers skated up to Devils goalie Martin Brodeur and started waving his hands and stick in front of the goalie's face. The distraction ploy worked, as Avery later scored, and the Rangers and won the series. The next day, the NHL amended their unsportsmanlike conduct rule to include the antics of Avery.

Furthermore, colorful baseball executive Bill Veeck recalled a ploy some Cubs fans used to upset their opponent. The team sold mirrors to fans at Wrigley Field, and Veeck wrote in his classic autobiography, *Veeck as in Wreck*, how women in the bleachers would often pull out the mirrors and attend to their makeup. He noted how odd it was that they only seemed to do this when the enemy was at bat—and, as he put it, "if a beam of light occasionally shone in the batter's eye on a particularly important pitch . . . well, what better pitch to choose?" He added that until this trick took place too often, it was "perfectly legal."

So again, barring some strange distraction, such as using a mirror or a laser pointer, what is happening in this basketball question would result in no action being taken by the referees. Now at the high school level, any such distractions are illegal. Refs would make sure fans ceased any distracting waving of banners, blaring of noisemakers, and so on. One high school ref stated that officials normally don't want to penalize a team for the actions of the crowd.

Be aware, though, that one rule does state that the actions of an opposing player trying to distract a foul shooter are another matter. It reads: "An opponent shall not disconcert the free thrower in any way, once the ball has been placed at the disposal of the shooter."

A memorable moment in NBA history happened during Game 1 of the 1997 Finals between the Chicago Bulls and the Utah Jazz. With nine seconds left in the game, Jazz forward Karl "The Mailman" Malone was at the free throw line with the score tied at 82–82. Before Malone was given the ball by the referee, Bulls forward Scottie Pippen was seen saying something to him. Malone, who had a career playoff free throw percentage of .736, missed both shots, and the Bulls grabbed the rebound with 7.5 seconds left. The Bulls got the ball immediately to Michael Jordan, who drained a jump shot with time expiring to clinch the win and take Game 1. The Bulls would end up winning the series, 4–2. After the game, broadcaster Jim Gray spoke with Scottie Pippen and asked him what he said to Malone before his free throws. Smiling, Pippen responded, "I said, 'The Mailman' doesn't deliver on Sundays."

(5) Clemson fans thought the play would result in them advancing the ball and getting it near their basket, but the Tigers were awarded the basketball back where the long pass had originated. Andre Young took a final pass and fired up a desperation shot from a spot near mid-court that made the home crowd gasp but just missed, as Maryland held on to win, 64–62.

(6) Officials ruled that there could be no goaltending on the play because the basketball had no chance of entering the cylinder of the hoop. It took some time to clear things up. It even appeared as if Kelly may have been fouled on the shot, but Duke was given two points on the Zeller tip-in. By the way, in such cases, the points are awarded to the offensive team's closest man to the play, not necessarily to the shooter.

The Kelly play helped the Blue Devils stay close and, shortly thereafter, go ahead to clinch a victory. Duke nailed down the win on an "I've-got-ice-water-running-through-my-veins" step back three-pointer by freshman Austin Rivers, son of former NBA star and current coach of the Boston Celtics Doc Rivers. His long jumper over the looming figure of Zeller left his fingertips with about 1.2 seconds remaining on the game clock and rattled in with absolutely no time showing on the scoreboard. It was his sixth trey on the evening and his 27th, 28th, and 29th points (good for a career single-game high). The buzzer beater capped the Blue Devils' 85–84 win, one that snapped North Carolina's school record of 31 consecutive victories on their home court. Rivers's 29 also represented the most points any Duke freshman has ever scored against a UNC squad.

It truly did take every single one of Duke's points scored over their 13–2 run to pull this one out. As a matter of fact, the only time Duke led in the second half was actually a split second after the clock hit zero—winning in effect, but not literally, *after* the game was over.

(7) The Wisconsin versus Michigan State contest of January 3, 2012, was a good example of what determines when time has run out. Wisconsin wound up losing the game when a Ryan Evans three-point bank shot in overtime was waved off by officials. Had the shot counted, Wisconsin would have pushed the game into a second overtime. Bedlam ensued over the call, which was made after an official review of the play. Badger coach Bo Ryan and the Madison, Wisconsin, crowd were apoplectic, but the rules concerning the official time are clearly delineated. It is the duty of an official at the scorers' table to keep track of the time left in a game, and the official clock is, as a rule but not always, connected to (and in sync with) the scoreboard clock that fans, players, and coaches can readily view.

At some levels of play, officials are assisted by a timing device they wear called PTS (Precision Timing System). The device allows officials to start and stop the game clock with a high degree of accuracy. In any event, the correct answer to this question has to be

"D" ("other"). Forget, for example, any clocks that are on display and may be in conflict—it's the official time, kept at the table, that counts.

The problem here is the discrepancy between clocks at the Wisconsin-Michigan State game. When the clock near the hoop read 00.0, the clock on the scoreboard was just about to switch from displaying 00.2 to 00.1, and it still showed one-tenth of a second left as the ball began its flight.

8 What Syracuse did on this play is legal if they executed it after a score. Passing to a teammate behind the endline is fine. Of course, this action can't take too long—the time limit alluded to in this question is five seconds.

Anthony, it should be noted, was just the third freshman ever to be selected as the Most Outstanding Player for an NCAA Final Four.

9 The dunk shot was outlawed, and the ban lasted exactly nine years, being lifted in time for the 1976–1977 season. The shot was declared illegal several months before Alcindor was to play his sophomore season. As mentioned, back then freshmen weren't permitted to play on the varsity squad, so 1967 would be the big stage debut for the star center who, at a fraction of an inch under 7' 2", could, when unimpeded by a rule, dunk with ease. Players such as Alcindor were still permitted to soar above the rim and could still place their hands *near* the rim, but they were now not allowed to slam the ball through the hoop. The best they could do was sort of drop the ball through the rim, just so long as their hand(s) didn't enter the imaginary cylindrical area extending up from the hoop.

By the way, it would take some time before the college ranks saw a woman dunk, legally or otherwise. The first woman to dunk during a game at the college level was West Virginia's Georgeann Wells, who stood 6' 7". She managed this feat on December 21, 1984, versus Charleston. At the pro level, Lisa Leslie of the Los Angeles Sparks would follow with her first WNBA dunk, occurring on July 30, 2002.

A final trivia note on dunking:

The man credited as being the first college player to dunk (in 1945) was Bob "Foothills" Kurland who, interestingly enough, didn't even play basketball until he was in high school. He is also considered to be basketball's first 7'0" player (although he later confessed that his college coach, Hank Iba, had fudged on his listed height by an inch and a half for psychological reasons). Kurland was also the first man to win the Most Outstanding Player trophy in the NCAA Tournament two years running. The three-time All-American did this while playing for Oklahoma A&M (now known as Oklahoma State). He led his Aggies to the national title in the 1945 tournament, topping New York University. The following year, they won it all again, this time defeating North Carolina.

As for Alcindor, some say the no-dunk rule may have made him become a better player, as he certainly did

LEW ALCINDOR

have—and continued to refine—many moves around the hoop beyond simply dunking the ball. Al Skinner, who played for UMass when Dr. J was there during the no-dunk era, commented that "There are tremendous advantages to not dunking the ball. It forces you to develop an interior game." Alcindor often relied upon finesse rather than sheer force to score, and his skyhook, an offspring of the dunking ban, was nearly impossible to defend. Released from a great height, it seemed as if this shot could not be blocked without the use of super-human force and/or without committing goaltending.

In 1966–1967, Lew Alcindor guided his UCLA Bruins to their second unbeaten season (30–0) in four years and its third national title over a four-year span. That season, he absolutely sizzled with a field goal percentage of .667, meaning he canned two of every three shots he put up (or, sometimes more accurately, shots he put *down*, using his hook and his height). His .667 mark represented the highest field goal percentage in the annals of the game. It seemed evident that no rule change could stop this man or the '66–'67 Bruins, a team that was selected as the top college hoop team of all time by the *Sporting News*.

For the record, Alcindor went on to capture three national titles while averaging 26.4 ppg. to go with his 15.5 rebounds each time he took to the court. UCLA ended up posting a lustrous 88–2 record over his ten-ure. He was the key member of the 1967–1968 squad that continued a winning streak from the year before to 47 consecutive games, and he even swept the NCAA

Tournament's Most Outstanding Player award in each of his three seasons as a Bruin.

(10) Allen made his claim that Chamberlain would shoot 100 percent from the free throw line because he actually had plans for Chamberlain to shoot below—that is to say, from *inside*—the foul line. He envisioned Chamberlain taking a running start toward the foul line, presumably from somewhere inside the midcourt circle, soaring from behind the free throw line, sailing through the air, and dunking every one of his foul shots. As a matter of fact, nba.com states that he could "leap with the ball from behind the foul line to deposit the ball in the basketball." He was able to jump the 15 feet from the line to the rim to complete his dunk free throws. The NCAA rule makers acted quickly and said players would be required to have their feet behind the free throw line at the time the ball was released from their hand. Needless to say, from that moment on, Chamberlain's chances for free throw superiority were dashed, and he continued to struggle with his "normal" foul shots.

Some other college players have since come along who, although not perfect from the charity stripe, were considered to be almost "automatic" on their free throw attempts. Take Duke's J. J. Redick, for example, who was so deadly from the foul line that when he missed a shot, Blue Devils fans were aghast, while opponents reacted as if they had just beheld a miracle. Redick finished a stellar 2003–2004 season with a .953 free throw percentage that, amazingly, was the third best in the history of NCAA play yet was only the second highest percentage *for that season*, 22 percentage points lower than the top man in this realm. The best from the line that year was Blake Ahearn of Missouri State, whose .975 set a new NCAA single season record. Ahearn's career free throw percentage of .946 also ranks as the best-ever in NCAA history, and he not only led the NCAA in free throw shooting three straight seasons, but twice rattled off streaks in which he sank sixty consecutive foul shots.

A final interesting note on Chamberlain: Although he may have drawn a multitude of fouls over his 14-year career—which covered 1,045 games—he never once fouled out of a contest.

(11) The violation for guiding the ball is simply considered to be offensive goaltending.

(12) Originally, the area around the free throw circle and the lane was called the key for a very good reason: It truly did resemble a key, because the lane back then was much more narrow than it is today, so it looked like the thin part of a key, and the free throw circle resembled the part people hold in turning the key.

The width of the lane—the area in which an offensive player may camp out for no longer than three seconds—was changed in the pros from being six feet across to a whopping 12 feet for the 1951–1952 season to figuratively shackle big man George Mikan, who checked in at 6' 10", making him a leviathan back then. Prior to the change, Mikan could legally settle himself in at a spot down low, never more than a few feet from the hoop, before making a move or before taking a short, high percentage shot.

The NBA widened the lane once more, going from 12 to 16 feet for the 1964–65 season, and that change was attributed to Chamberlain. Many people around the league felt he was simply *too* dominant, so they tried to hamper him a bit. Realizing Chamberlain controlled the lane with impunity, they were attempting to prevent him from entrenching himself close to the hoop.

Now it's been said that the lane was likewise widened in college ball because of Bill Russell, who averaged 20.3 rebounds per game and 20.7 ppg. throughout his college career. His team went 28–1 to secure the national title in 1954-55, and, despite the rule change, the Dons posted an untarnished 29–0 record and another national title the following season—not bad for a guy who didn't make his Oakland, California, high school team as a 6' 2", 128-pound sophomore and who was only good enough to be a third-stringer in his junior year.

According to hickoksports.com, the NCAA instituted "Russell's Rules," which not only called for the widening of the lane, but also made it "illegal for a player to touch the ball when it's on its downward arc to the basket."[2]

---

[2] The original goaltending rule in college dates back to 1945 due to the influence of Bob Kurland.

"Doggie" Julian, a college coach and a member of the Rules Committee, stated that "We weren't planning to make any changes, but after some of the coaches saw Russell's [tournament] performance, they got scared."

 13 Two-time Patriot League player of the year McCollum was awarded two foul shots, and Lehigh maintained possession of the ball after the free throws. The Mountain Hawks had gained the lead with 8:21 to play, and they never again relinquished it.

Going into this contest, a 15th-ranked school had bumped off a number 2 seed just four times since the tournament was expanded to 16 seeds per region in 1985. However, on this day of upsets, the rarity happened twice, with Norfolk State having earlier shocked Missouri. ESPN reported that early that day, there were 4,728 perfect brackets left of the 6.45 million that had been filled out—and after the day's upsets, which included the number 13-seeded Ohio Bobcats knocking off Michigan (#4), not one person could still boast of a perfect bracket.

Duke coach Mike Krzyzewski noted of the loss to Lehigh: "today is one of those incredible lows." Despite the defeat, Coach K remains a legend, one whose impact on the Duke program is nearly immeasurable. To illustrate his impact, just take a glance at Duke's 1994–1995 season. Krzyzewski led his troops to a 9–3 record before health problems shelved him. His replacement could only muster a poor 4–15 record with the same players. When Krzyzewski returned, he was able to post a 24–9 record by the 1996–1997 season. He followed that up with a 32-win year before guiding Duke to a scorching hot 37–2 record the very next season, which included the first-ever perfect 16–0 season in the highly respected Atlantic Coast Conference (ACC).

He certainly has come a long way from the day he was hired as the Duke head coach. Virtually unknown back then, he was greeted on campus by a headline in the school newspaper that identified him as the new coach and added, alluding to the spelling of the new coach's last name, this message: "THIS IS NOT A TYPO."

(14) The NCAA shot clock now gives a men's team no more than 35 seconds before they must take a shot that, again, must at the very least strike iron. If a player got the shot off before the time expired, and that shot did, say, hit the rim, then there is no infraction.

The shot clock has changed over the years. At first it was set for 30 seconds (the same length of time the ABA would eventually use). The collegiate shot clock came into effect for the 1969–1970 season on an experimental basis for NCAA women's basketball and was then etched into the rulebook the following season. For men's basketball, the clock, initially a 45-second timer, was first used in 1985–1986. In the 1993–1994 season, the decision was made to go with a 35-second shot clock.

An 11–6 win by Tennessee over Temple in 1973 and coaching tactics such as freezing the ball (such as the 1956 game in which the University of California sat on the basketball against Bill Russell's USF Dons, doing so at one point for eight minutes while a motionless Joe Hagler simply held the ball) and Dean Smith's four-corner offense made the NCAA finally realize a shot clock simply had to be implemented.

By the way, on the other side of the freezing the ball issue was the run and gun style of play. When Loyola-Marymount played U.S. International on the final day of January in 1989, a point was put on the board every 7.3 seconds, and a shot went up, on average, every 10.9 seconds. The slugfest of a game ended with Loyola, who had four of Paul Westhead's players finish with more points than minutes played, ending up on top, 181–150, breaking the record for the highest scoring game in college ball. That record had been established twenty-four days earlier when the same two teams played pinball with the scoreboard to a tune of 162–144. Two years later, on January 5, 1991, Loyola trounced U.S. International, 186–140, giving them the record for the most points scored by one team in a single game.

15. A player inbounding has five seconds to release the basketball and get it in play.

16. There is no time limit for a player to pick up the basketball while it is rolling, as mentioned in this question. Of course, he has to secure the ball quickly if the defense puts pressure on him, and, naturally, there's a space limit as to how far a player can allow the ball to roll before it would trickle out of bounds.

On March 18, 2012, in the third round of the NCAA Tournament, Lehigh, down by seven points to Xavier, tried to save time by rolling the ball in with just 24.3 ticks left on the clock. The basketball traveled for seven seconds, almost making it all the way down to Lehigh's three-point arc before Mackey McKnight of the Mountain Hawks picked it up. Ultimately, Xavier advanced after prevailing in this one, 70–58.

(17) Lockhart was permitted to play on, but the rules state a player may not inbound the ball by either dribbling it in directly or by passing to himself. His only recourse was to throw the ball off an opposing player and then enter the playing area in an effort to recover the ball. His team had built up a 13-point lead before Lockhart's solo act commenced, and he actually was able to recover the ball several times. This seems like a fantastic and/or awfully lucky accomplishment. Weren't his opponents instructed to stay far away from him when he was trying the only ploy he had at his disposal? At any rate, he managed to sink five foul shots, kill some time, and ultimately hang on for the win. While outscored 10 to 5 down the stretch, his team still prevailed, 75–67.

In the NBA, a similar situation took place in 1952 during a Syracuse Nationals overtime game versus the Baltimore Bullets. When a member of the Nationals fouled out in overtime, it left the team with just four players. The refs decided to allow Syracuse to keep five players on the court, but they also ruled that every time a member of that team who had already fouled out committed another foul, Baltimore would be awarded technical foul shots on top of any other free throws they had coming to them. The game ended after eight Nationals fouled out and with Baltimore coming out on top, 97–91.

Back in 1949, a player named Don Otten fouled out of a game, but, as was the case above, he reentered the game when his Tri-Cities team got into massive foul trouble. He wound up committing eight fouls to set a new record, but his Blackhawks still managed to top Sheboygan, 120–113.

(18) Looking to stun UNC and become the first team seeded 13th or lower to advance to the regional finals since the NCAA Tournament expanded in 1985, the Bobcats began the overtime at a disadvantage because, yes, a team in the bonus or double bonus during regulation play stays that way in overtime. UNC would continue to shoot two free throws when they went to the line after being fouled by Ohio U.

As it turned out, this point was moot, as the Tar Heels ran off five consecutive points before the Bobcats, who would shoot 0-for-6 from the field in overtime, finally scored on two free throws with 1:34 to go. North Carolina eventually dashed Ohio's lofty dreams and upset hopes by the score of 73–65.

(19) No, this is basketball, not football. A handoff as described is not permitted.

(20) Award no bucket on this long distance pass/shot.

(21) Yes, refs can, in dire situations, declare a game to be over before the usual 40 minutes of play are completed. On December 10, 2011, a yearly crosstown rivalry between Xavier and Cincinnati went completely out of control when a bloody brawl broke out. The melee eventually resulted in eight players being suspended (including stiff six-game suspensions dished out to Cincinnati's Yancy Gates, Octavius Ellis, and Cheikh Mbodj). In addition, at the discretion of the officials, the 76–53 Musketeers victory came in a game that ended 9.4 seconds short of regulation play—in other words, the refs did not allow the game to resume after the fracas.

In June of 2012, the two schools agreed to move their annual game to a neutral court. Instead of holding their next two games on campus, they would continue their rivalry at a downtown Cincinnati arena in 2012 and 2013, with each team taking turns being the host team and with ticket sales being split between the two schools.

(22) It is not legal; it's a lane violation because a player cannot stand inside the three-point arc unless, of course, he's lined up along the lane, nor can he move into a position inside the arc before a foul shot strikes the iron. Remarkably, this infraction occurred twice in the 2012 NCAA Tournament. In fact, it happened in games just one day apart.

North Carolina-Asheville, giving Syracuse a real run for their money, was whistled for making this mistake on March 15, 2012. The call hurt their chances for becoming the first-ever number 16 seed to knock off a number 1 seed (continuing the streak of 109 straight losses of 16 seeds against 1 seeds). Although the Bulldogs led Syracuse for much of the game (they were only the third number 16 ever to hold a halftime lead against a number 1), they would ultimately fall short, 72–65.

The controversial lane violation call, one of two highly controversial calls against the Bulldogs late in the game, was made on J. P. Primm, the team's top scorer on the night (with 18). The call left Bulldogs coach Eddie Biedenbach livid, requiring an assistant to restrain him. With 1:20 left to play and with Scoop Jardine at the line, refs felt Primm was guilty of "passing the head of the key before Jardine let the shot [the first of a 1-and-1] go." He missed on the front end but was given a do-over because of the lane violation—nailing that shot as well as the second one to give the Orange a 64–58 lead.

Somehow Notre Dame's Jerian Grant didn't learn from the call on Primm. The very next day after Primm's violation, Grant was called for the same infraction, costing the Fighting Irish a chance to force Xavier into overtime. With a mere 2.8 seconds left in the game and with the Irish losing by two, Eric Atkins of Notre Dame sank the front end of a 1-and-1 when the whistle blew. Grant had "left his position behind the three-point arc too early, running in for a rebound before the ball hit the rim."

In another matter involving free throw violations, in the 2012 semifinal round, a shooter, Aaron Craft, got caught crossing the foul line prematurely, doing so as a strategic/desperation move. Trailing by three points to Kansas with 2.9 seconds to play, the Ohio State guard went to the line, where he sank his first shot to take the score to 64–62, Kansas. When he was given the basketball for his second shot, he almost instantaneously threw it off the front of the rim in an effort to catch Jayhawk players napping. He hoped to rebound his own shot and stick it back in to send the game into overtime. Although he did grab the rebound, his timing was off just a bit, and the refs nabbed him. Seconds later, with the Buckeyes out of timeouts, Kansas easily killed the clock to advance to the title game.

Oddly, this game represented just the second matchup of number 2 seeds since the seeding process began in 1979.

(23) Such plays take place, though not too often. In the 2012 NCAA Tournament, several players from both Xavier and Baylor were going after a ball. Because many flying hands took swipes at the ball until it was finally batted out of bounds, the officials, who probably were screened from seeing the action well and were not quite sure just whose fingertip had caused the basketball to leave the court, were stymied. Two of them huddled to verify that neither one had seen the play clearly, then, in effect, treated the play as if it were a jump ball. The team with the possession arrow going their way is given the ball in such situations.

(24) The team with the possession arrow pointing their way gets the ball. The rules regarding the arrow have eliminated many situations that used to call for jump balls, such as when two opposing players become, in effect, wrestlers and tie up the ball. Likewise, young fans no doubt have no recollection of jump balls to, say, begin the action of the second half of games.

(25) In this case, the refs didn't see the infraction, but the proper call here is goaltending. As longtime (30+ years) high school official Mark Pena noted, "When the ball is in the cylinder, nobody can touch the rim or the net. If Team B [the team on defense, without the ball] interferes when a two-point goal is shot, award two points, and award three if it is a three-point attempt." Of course, if a player from Team A interferes, no goal is awarded.

On this play, Lamb would have had a chance for a three-point play had the call been made. As it was, he converted both free throws. Ultimately, it didn't matter, as Kentucky won, 67–59, to capture their eighth national title.[3] The Wildcats wound up with 38 wins on the season, the most ever in the annals of men's Division I basketball.

They also wound up becoming the only college team ever to have players selected number one and two in

---

[3] Only UCLA with 11 has more.

the draft, freshmen Anthony Davis and Michael-Kidd Gilchrist. The school also tied a record with six players taken overall.

(26) Easy call, "B," foul on Craft. There once was an option to call a force-out on such plays, but no more. In the NBA, for example, the rule involving force-outs was clarified before the 1974–1975 season (calling a force-out "incidental contact near a boundary line, which causes a player to commit a violation or go out of bounds, and neither team is responsible for the action. The offensive team retains possession"). The NBA must not have liked the rule too much, as the force-out was dropped prior to the 1976–1977 season.

By the way, the teams of the 2012 Final Four featured plenty of players who had famous relatives. Ohio State's Shannon Scott's father is former NBA star Charlie Scott; Kentucky's Marquis Teague's brother Jeff plays for the Atlanta Hawks, and his teammate Terrence Jones has ex-NBA star Damon Stoudamire as a cousin; Louisville's Chris Smith's older brother J.R. is with the New York Knicks, while Mark Jackson, Jr. is the son of NBA standout and current coach of the Golden State Warriors, Mark Jackson. As for the champion Kentucky Wildcats, Justin Wesley has two brothers, Keith and Kevin Langford, who played in the NBA, and Christian Garrett is the cousin of UCLA football great Mike Garrett, who went on to play in the NFL. Garrett is also the cousin of major league baseball star Chris Chambliss.

27 There's nothing illegal here—teams do this all the time. Here is the way to determine if there is an over and back violation: First of all, this call is never to be made unless an "offensive player has crossed the half-court line offensively with both feet and the ball." The keys here, and this is the point that confuses many fans, are the words *both* and *and*—the player *and* the ball must have gone over midcourt and with *both* feet. Additionally, the infraction only occurs if that player then crosses "back onto the defensive side of the court with the ball" and does so with "either foot or the ball" going over the midcourt line.

28 Before the arrow possession, which is, of course, used under the alternating possession rule, a jump ball between the two men struggling over the ball would result when the ball was tied up. The alternating possession rule came to the college ranks in 1981.

Back in the Dark Age of basketball, a jump ball took place after every made basket. For that matter, a person (at first a janitor who sat on a ladder) posted by the hoop had to pluck the ball out of the peach basket after each and every score in the days before nets were attached to the rim. The center jump after every score was eliminated in 1937.

29 The answer here is no. A player may not use this tactic under *any* circumstances, as was the phrasing for this question. He may run the baseline in many cases, but not from a dead ball situation.

(30) As the ref you would hit the team with a technical foul. The most famous instance of this rule coming into play was, of course, the time Chris Webber of Michigan did this in the 1993 championship game versus North Carolina. The Wolverines were behind by two with 11 seconds to go when he signaled for a timeout his team didn't have, and UNC went on to win, 77–71.

Webber was, of course, a big part of Michigan's "Fab Five," a group that also included Jalen Rose, Jimmy King, Juwan Howard, and Ray Jackson. With that crew, Michigan became the first team in the annals of NCAA play to make it to the title game of the tournament with five freshman starters.

(31) Something was done, but not much. League officials agreed that the refs had been wrong and had probably cost the Bearcats a victory. However, they also ruled that Cincinnati's defeat would stand.

(32) The officiating crew declared the shot to be good, awarding a 65–63 win to Drake. As you may recall from the introduction to this book, way back in 1895, backboards were first introduced to the sport because rule makers felt they would prevent "fans from interfering with play," especially those baskets that were hung on balconies. Well . . . the backboards didn't hinder this particular Wichita State fan, but his actions cost his team a chance for victory.

(33) Over the years, the field of teams selected to play in the NCAA Tournament has changed quite a bit. For example, in 1952, it was announced that the tourney would expand from 16 to 22 teams. Now, a whopping 68 teams go to "the dance," counting the teams that must take part in play-in games in order to advance to the field of 64.

OTHER LEVELS OF BASKETBALL

For the purpose of this chapter, the words "other levels of basketball" will include women's competitions, even if a given question deals with college ball.

(1) Let's start with a women's basketball game from February 2012, one that took place in Nebraska. The women from Burke took part in a charity contest held on their home court, and they wore pink uniforms to pay tribute to the Make-A-Wish Foundation. At the start of the second half, the opposing Columbus team was down by a point. Their coach, Dave Licari, told the officials that the home team was required by rule to wear white uniforms. What, if any, punishment was assessed for this rules violation?

Answer on page 133

(2) You're working a high school game, and a coach points out that the players on the other team are wearing uniforms with numbers that don't match up with the numbers next to their names in the official scorebook. What do you do here—is there some action you'd take to rectify the situation? Is any sort of penalty called for with a mix-up involving numbers?

Answer on pages 133–135

(3) What is the proper call if a high school player is caught dunking the ball during warm-ups?

Answer on page 135

(4) Back in 1972, one of the most embarrassing stains on the refereeing profession took place during the Olympic Games held in Munich, Germany. The United States basketball team, showcasing such standouts as Tom McMillen, Doug Collins, and Bobby Jones, was moments away from earning another gold medal when the outrageous event(s) unfolded.

First, some background. From 1936 (the first year basketball became an Olympic sport) up to 1972, teams from the United States had won seven consecutive gold medals, breezing to an untarnished 63–0 record and winning games with ease, often coasting to their inevitable gold medal. In 1972, they outscored their opponents by a margin of nearly 23 points despite their one defeat. They won their games leading up to their final contest by these scores: 66–35, 81–55, 67–48, and a rare squeaker, 61–54, against Brazil. Following that close match came a romp over Egypt in which they more than tripled their opponent's point total, 96–31. Next came scores of 72–56 versus Spain, another drubbing, 99–33, this one versus Japan, and a 68–38 win in the semifinals over Italy. Winning had come to be expected by everyone.

All that was about to change.

Matched against a talented team from the USSR and playing them for the gold (the fifth time doing so in the history of the games), the US floundered. They trailed by five points at the half and were down by as many as 10 in the second half. However, they scratched back and eventually took a 50–49 lead with just three seconds left in the game on two foul shots by Collins after he had been mugged—undercut by a defender—on an attempted layup. A still-dazed Collins had managed to get up from the floor and sink both of his shots, even though the horn went off "in the middle of his second attempt." Collins said the horn sounded when the Russians were attempting to call a timeout, but in that situation, calling a timeout was not permitted. Thus, the refs ignored the horn, and after the second shot went down, one ref signaled for play to continue.

Then with that precious little amount of time left on the clock, the Soviet team got the ball inbounds but couldn't score as time nearly expired. Victory for legendary coach Hank Iba and his team was, it certainly seemed, assured.

Not quite.

Even though the ref from Bulgaria had, in fact, signaled for play to begin after the second made free throw, the official from Brazil blew his whistle not long after the ball had been put in play by the USSR—when they had advanced the ball near midcourt with still one second left on the scoreboard. He did so "after hearing the earlier horn and [then soon after] seeing a disturbance near the scorer's table." The Soviets contended they had signaled for a timeout before Collins had taken his foul shots. Now it seemed the frantic Soviets still wanted to use a timeout.

One American player would later say that a Soviet coach had been running along the sideline trying to get that timeout called. That act of leaving the bench, said the American, should have resulted in a technical foul being called. No foul was assessed, but play did come to a halt.

According to one source, Dr. William Jones, the head of the FIBA (the International Basketball Federation) from Great Britain, then made a ruling that the clock be reset once more, this time for three seconds with the Russians again retaining the ball back on the baseline. Sources also say that Jones did not have the authority to make such a ruling, but that point now, sadly, is moot.

Eventually, the refs did order that the clock be reset for three seconds, but as their orders were being carried out, the referees prematurely put the ball in play. An extremely long shot, taken almost immediately after the inbound pass was received, went off target as the buzzer sounded. Time had apparently run out, and the USA players, coaches, and tons of fans stormed the court, beginning to celebrate their win as they had captured the gold.

Once more it was a case of not-so-fast.

The players—in the middle of a plethora of chaos—were instructed that the clock had never been reset (that's why the buzzer had sounded so soon after the last inbound pass) and the game would, therefore, commence again with three ticks left to play and with the Soviet team in control of the ball.

A writer from the *New York Times* later wrote, "It began to look as if the officials would give the Russians the extra [time] for as long as it took them to shoot the winning field goal."

The Russians did win it, 51–50, scoring on their third try. A length-of-the-court pass from Ivan Edeshko hit Aleksander Belov, who had two defenders—Kevin Joyce and Jim Forbes—draped on him in the lane. They "went up for the ball, but the Americans were knocked off by Belov, who suddenly found himself with an incredibly easy layup." The game-winning bucket was, in effect, uncontested because the refs did not see, or, some say, chose not to call, a foul on Belov for warding off the defenders, "sending the two Americans sprawling." Nor did they notice, as some have asserted, that the passer had stepped on the baseline during his desperation heave. From the perspective of the American team, the officials, determined to aid the Soviet squad, had prevailed.

Now, here's your question: As is the case with baseball when a manager exercises his right to play a game under protest, was the USA team permitted to file a protest, or, under Olympic rules, was the word (and were the calls) of the refs final in this matter?

Answer on pages 135–136

(5) Baylor star Brittney Griner, who stands at 6′ 8″ and became just the second woman ever to dunk in NCAA Tournament play, led her team to a win over Pat Summitt's

BRITTNEY GRINER

Tennessee women's team on March 26, 2012, thanks to her 23 points, 15 rebounds, and nine blocked shots. The win propelled the Lady Bears to a 38–0 record and into the Final Four.

At the 46.8 mark in the second half, Baylor's guard Odyssey Sims fell to the floor, where she and Vols leading scorer, Shekinna Stricklen, skirmished and had to be pulled apart. Nobody threw a punch, but Griner and two other Lady Bears left the bench. What punishment was doled out for their actions under NCAA rules?

Answer on pages 136–137

6 Yes or No: Is the distance from the three-point arc to the hoop the same for both men and women in NCAA competition?

Answer on page 137

7 How does a ref determine if a player's position was such that he or she shot from behind the arc? If a player was, say, standing with one foot behind the three-point line but had his or her other foot in the air over the line as he or she jumped toward the hoop to get off the shot, does the player get two or three points for his or her bucket? Just what is the key on such calls?

Answer on pages 137–138

8 The ABA began play by trying to differentiate itself from the NBA. Remember the old ABA? The league that under first commissioner George Mikan utilized the three-point shot and the red, white, and blue basketball? Well, test

your memory of its rules from their final season. The ABA instituted a "no foul-out rule," no doubt figuring that fans don't pay to see games in which their favorite player might have to sit out a good portion of a game due to foul trouble and/or disqualifications. However, after a player committed his sixth personal foul, any additional fouls he was whistled for resulted in what consequences?

Answer on page 138

⑨ Here's a yes or no question about the FIBA rulebook: is it within the rules for a player to touch the ball immediately once it has struck the rim? Specifically, say a player from the United States takes a shot that hits the rim, bounces up, and appears as if it will fall back down into the hoop, but an opposing player slaps it away before it has a chance to drop back down. Is this legal?

Answer on pages 138–140

⑩ Thanks to a 1989 change in the rules the Olympics follow, NBA players were finally permitted to compete for the gold. Your challenge is to recall the first time this took place. In what year did refs have to make calls with so many formidable players on the court (the year in which the original members of the Dream Team captured gold medals in Barcelona)?

Answer on pages 140–141

⑪ Members of that Dream Team were clearly the best players in the world, but they didn't look as recognizable in their jerseys to most fans as they did in their NBA

DAVID ROBINSON

uniforms due to a rule that seems very foreign to most Americans. Only certain jersey numbers were legal in Olympic play, so Michael Jordan, for example, was not wearing his familiar #23. List, if you can, five of the 12 numbers that players could don in international play under FIBA rules.

Answer on page 141

(12) In the Olympics, how much time does a team have to cross midcourt with the ball?

Answer on page 141

(13) True or false: In the Olympics, only a head coach or one of his assistants may call a timeout.

Answer on page 141

(14) How many fouls does it take to disqualify an Olympic basketball player?

Answer on page 142

(15) Back to high school basketball. When Wilt Chamberlain was playing for Overbrook High School, a play was drawn up to utilize his huge height advantage. The plan was for a teammate to inbound the ball from underneath the Overbrook hoop by lofting it over the backboard. Chamberlain was to leap, grab the pass, and dunk or lay it in for an easy two points. Was this play legal?

Answer on page 142

(16) Forward Richard Mudd played in the Continental Basketball League (CBL) for the Detroit Spirits. In a contest against Evansville, Mudd pulled down a rebound off the defensive boards but, apparently all mixed up, stuck it back in the other team's basket. What's the ruling in such rare cases? Would you declare a dead ball and award the ball to Evansville? Does the score count, or would the ball remain live with both teams eligible to battle for it once again?

Answer on page 142

(17) Is there a limit to the amount of technical fouls a player or coach can be accessed before he is ejected from a game?

Answer on page 142

(18) Is it possible to forfeit a game before it has even begun? If so, name one or two ways in which this can occur.

Answer on pages 142–143

(19) In 2011, an odd play took place between two high schools in Maine. Your job is to determine if a basket counted or not. Tyler Lyle of Sacopee Valley had the ball near his own hoop, trying to inbound the ball. After considering several options on the pass in, he wound up firing a bounce pass. The ball hit the floor, ricocheted off a player from A.R. Gould, and went through the hoop. Is Sacopee Valley awarded two points, or is the basket waived off?

Answer on page 143

JUMP BALL BETWEEN
ANTHONY DAVIS
AND DWIGHT HOWARD

20 You're a high school ref about to work a girls' basketball game. Let's say you're checking out the equipment before the start of the contest and notice the game basketball is the same one that was used in the boys' game held just the night before. Is there a problem here?

Answer on page 143

21 Two players square off for a jump ball. The ref throws the ball off line, much closer to one player than the other, giving that player an advantage—or let's say the ref felt he had thrown the ball too high and had messed up the mechanics of the jump ball. He decides to stop play and call for a rejump. Can a coach call for a different player to take part in the rejump or not?

Answer on page 143

22 Team A is about to inbound the ball in. A player from Team B reaches through the imaginary boundary plane and makes contact with the basketball before the ball has been released from the passer's hands. Under the National Federation of State High School Associations's (NFHS) rules, is there a penalty for such actions? If so, what exactly is the penalty?

Answer on page 145

23 Explain the difference between the NCAA rule and the NFHS rule involving when the clock is stopped on a made basket.

Answer on page 145

REFEREE SHELLY MANGRUM

ANSWERS

(1) Game officials slapped Burke with a technical foul and gave Columbus two free throws. Columbus eventually went on to win by a score of 62–47.

There are times when rules are so petty. A Florida school (T.F. South) was hit with a technical foul before their game on December 2, 2011, for wearing uniforms that were declared "illegal" because they broke a new rule prohibiting letters (in this case, two of the letters that spelled out the name of the school above each player's jersey number) from being closer than an inch to the number. It turned out, in this case, that the two foul shots made on the technical foul had no bearing in the T.F. South win. Furthermore, after later inspection, it also turned out that the uniforms were, in fact, legal. It almost seems like refs should be equipped not only with whistles, but rulers, as well. Soon after, new rules intended to make things easier for refs to spot uniform numbers more readily during games were put on the books.

(2) There are many rules involving uniforms and numbers. For example, the NFHS, which regulates the official rules involving high school basketball play, addresses scorebook issues. Their rules state that teams must submit the names and numbers of their starters and other possible players for a given game to the officials at the scorers' table no later than 10 minutes prior to game time. Failure to do this results in a technical foul.

Under NFHS rules, after the 10-minute deadline passes, "a single additional technical foul is charged to the team regardless of how many of the following are committed . . .," and they go on to mention infractions such as changing/correcting a player's number in the scorebook, inserting another player's name to the team list, and having "identical numbers on team members or players."

Therefore, the answer to this question is simple— having the players in the game while wearing incorrect jersey numbers results in a technical foul being leveled against the offending team.

The NFHS has other rules involving uniforms, including the one that mandates that the home team wear white jerseys, that no player wear jewelry, and that any headband or wristband worn by a player be of a solid color.

3 Without going into too much depth, the penalty is this: the offending player from Team A is hit with a "T" for dunking during warm-ups, and the game will begin with a player from the opposing team taking two shots for the technical foul. His team will also get the ball to begin the game (but the possession arrow will then be pointed toward the bucket of the team that had been guilty of pregame dunk).

4 The USA did protest this debacle (twice, actually) but did so fully expecting they would lose their appeal. In fact, before the five-man jury came to its decision, the dejected, disillusioned, and bitter American players, convinced that they were the best team of the 124 squads competing, voted to reject the silver medal for their second-place finish. It marked the first time that a team or athlete had refused an Olympic medal.

Sure enough, the jury, which included three representatives from Communist bloc countries who all voted against the Americans, let the shameful performance by the officials and the win for the Soviets stand.

As a postscript, one member of the USA team, Kenneth Davis, was so irate at the decision that he had an article placed in his will ordering that his descendants never accept the silver medal offered to him. He and his teammates believed that they had earned a medal, but it was one of gold, not silver.

Collins, however, wound up with a gold medal, and in a most unusual way. His son, Chris, was a coach for the USA Olympic basketball team in 2008, and although coaches aren't awarded the official medals, the chairman for USA basketball, Jerry Colangelo, arranged for replica gold medals to be provided for the coaching staff. Chris, teary-eyed, presented his medal to his father. After nearly four decades, Doug Collins proudly wore a gold medal around his neck.

5 The three women who left the bench were ejected, not really a stinging punishment given the little amount of time left in the game. The NCAA stated none of the players involved would be suspended for any Final Four action. In the NBA, if a player leaves the bench, it results in an automatic suspension.

The next day, it was announced that Griner, a junior who had helped Baylor to its second Final Four in three seasons, was a unanimous selection for The Associated Press All-America team. For the record, Baylor won it all, going 40–0 on the season and becoming the first team in NCAA history to win 40 games. They also became the seventh women's team to post a perfect season, joining Connecticut (with four of their Huskies teams achieving this feat), Tennessee, and Texas. The dominating Griner, not at all surprisingly, was named the Most Outstanding Player of the tourney.

(6) The distance from the arc to the hoop, defined as the distance from "the center of the basket to the outside edge of the three-point field-goal line," was moved from 19′ 9″ to 20′ 9″ before the 2011–2012 season began. As for the men, their rule makers had added a foot to the old distance of 19′ 9″ back on May 3, 2007. So, yes, the rule/distance is the same now for both women and men in college ball, while it has remained at 19′ 9″ at the high school and middle school levels.

(7) The rule here clearly does apply to both men and women, and it states that a player is considered to be outside/beyond the three-point line when he or she has "at least one foot in contact with the playing floor behind

the line before the release of the try [field goal attempt] and the other foot not contacting the line or the playing floor in the front of the line." Furthermore, if a player takes a shot while leaping, his/her position is considered to be what it was when he/she was "last in contact with the floor . . ."; therefore, the three-point attempt counts (assuming that both feet of the shooter were behind the line before that player jumped).

(8) The team that was fouled by an ABA player who already had six fouls on him was given two free throws, and they maintained possession of the basketball—an odd but interesting rule.

(9) Yes, this is legal. Likewise, a fellow USA player would be permitted to grab the ball once it had hit the rim and, say, cram it back in for a score. So yes, an opponent could slap the basketball away after it had touched the iron even if it was still within the imaginary cylinder extending up from the hoop. That held true even if the ball was, say, resting on the rim and ready to drop for a basket.

When the United States lost in the 2004 Olympics to Argentina, one website, cbc.ca, reported that our players "were dumbfounded as Argentinean big men Luis Scola and Fabricio Oberto flicked many of their shots—and free throws—off the rim." One observer noted it is difficult for "North Americans to figure it out first time around. You kind of freeze as if expecting the ref to make the call."

KARIMA CHRISTMAS

Some American players have had trouble adjusting to such rules—alien to our game—when playing in the Olympics. Certainly American players must have felt odd when they used to line up for free throw shots along a lane that tapered, going from being quite wide at the baseline to a more narrow distance across at the free throw line. Thus, it was shaped like a trapezoid and not a rectangle.

More significant (if memory serves correctly), after turnovers, foreign players knew that they didn't have to check the ball with refs, and they would quickly start new plays, sometimes catching opponents in vulnerable moments of unpreparedness. In the meantime, the American players—trained otherwise—looked for a ref to hand the ball to before they would inbound to begin their attack. This, of course, slowed down their game.

Finally, again according to cbc.ca, international rules permit an offensive player to "clear out space for a shot with his free arm," a move NBA players normally avoid, for fear of getting called for an offensive foul. Plus, if an American defender, playing under, say, NBA rules, touches the offensive player's arm as he uses it to clear out space, he will get called for a foul.

(10) The year was 1992, and the magnificent team from the United States crushed its opponents by an average of 44 points per game. That team featured, to name just five of its illustrious dozen stars, Michael Jordan, Larry Bird, Magic Johnson, Karl Malone, and Charles Barkley. The

only college player on the roster (and non hall of famer) was Duke's Christian Laettner.

According to nba.com, "Opponents didn't have a chance, but they didn't care. One player, while trying to guard Magic Johnson, was seen frantically waving to a camera-wielding teammate on the bench, signaling to make sure he got a picture of them together."

⑪ Legal numbers are 4 through 15. Jordan wore #9.

There was a time when players at some levels of basketball were not allowed to wear a number higher than 55. The reasoning for this was simple—after a player committed a foul, refs would signal which player was guilty of the infraction to the scorekeeper. The ref would, for example, indicate a player wearing number 23 by holding up two digits on one hand, the hand he always used for the "10s" units, for the "20" part of the number, and three fingers on his other hand, which he used to signify the "ones" units, for the "3" part of the number. Hence, using one flash of his fingers, he could hold up to the maximum of five fingers on each hand to indicate #55 had committed a foul.

⑫ A team has eight seconds to advance the ball into the frontcourt.

⑬ False. The only person who is permitted to call a timeout is the head coach.

(14) It takes just five fouls for a player to find himself on the bench for the duration of a game.

(15) It was legal and quite easy for Chamberlain to execute.

(16) The basketball went through the Evansville hoop in this case, so give them two points under the rules of the league.

(17) Yes, there is a limit, but listen to the tale of a coach who amassed 12 technical fouls before he actually exited the game. In a 1979 match between Notre Dame High School and a Los Angles high school named Daniel Murphy, the Notre Dame team held a 67–61 lead when their coach, Glen Marx, went ballistic. After arguing and picking up three technical fouls, he was supposed to depart from the court but refused. Frustrated referees kept heaping more Ts on Marx, but he dug in his heels until the last of the 12 techs was called on him. Herb Simon of Daniel Murphy toed the line, sank 11 of his 12 foul shots, and Notre Dame wound up on the losing end of things, 72–67. Obstinacy and anger took what appeared to be a sure win and turned it into a tally mark in the loss column.

(18) It would take something drastic to forfeit a game under any circumstances, but it *can* happen, even before the opening tipoff. According to highschoolrivals.com, a 2006 high school game in Montana resulted in just such a forfeiture. The website stated the rule thusly:

"If a backboard is damaged by a pregame dunk, the offending school must forfeit," and that's just what happened to the boys' team from Harlem, Montana. Other ways are if a team refuses to take the court, the team doesn't have enough players, the officials feel that there's danger for the athletes or fans, as well as other situations.

19 The basket counts, as there is no rule against it.

20 The regulation size basketball for boys' games has a circumference between 29 1/2 and 30 inches, but girls use a smaller ball, one that is permitted to be between 28 1/2 and 29 inches in circumference. So, yes, there is a problem with the ball in this question. Most refs would simply ask for a correct ball to be found. If, for whatever reason, a girls' ball could not be located, a good ref with a modicum of common sense would probably allow the game to go on using the boys' basketball. Referee Mark Pena added that if play had begun before someone noticed the boys' ball was being used, once that was "detected you change to the correct ball at the point of interruption. All points count, no penalty, play on."

21 Unlike the rules of the NCAA, which permit any two players to take part in a rejump, NFHS rules state the two players who were involved in the original jump ball must be the ones used for the rejump.

**USA BASKETBALL
COACH CHUCK DALY**

22 Yes, there is a penalty. The official rules state a technical foul would be charged and "a throw-in boundary-plane warning is assessed."

23 The clock is to be stopped in NCAA action after a made basket "in the last minute of the second half or in the last minute of overtime." On the other hand, NFHS rules have no rule requiring the clock to be stopped after any made basket.

MERCEDES RUSSELL

BONUS QUESTIONS

Here are new, updated questions added to this, the second edition of *You're the Basketball Ref*. The level of difficulty varies, so there should be something for everyone, from the casual fan to hardcore rules experts.

(1) On March 8, 2018, Duke was pitted against Notre Dame in the quarterfinals of the ACC tournament. About halfway through the first half, Alex O'Connell fed Duke standout Marvin Bagley III with a wraparound pass. Bagley, who was primed to spring high for a sure dunk, was being guarded down low by Austin Torres. Bagley had Torres on his right hip as he spun to his left, to the hoop. Out of position, the 6' 7" Torres grabbed Bagley around the shoulders in desperation as the 6' 11" ACC Player of the Year made his move. Torres tugged on Bagley, causing him to hit the deck. The refs instantly called the foul.

Your easy question: under NCAA rules, can officials decide that they want to take a look at such a play to determine if it should be considered a flagrant foul?

Answer on page 155

(2) The Grizzlies and Suns were tied at 97 with .6 seconds to play in a game held the day after Christmas in 2017. Phoenix took the ball out of bounds next to a hash mark

by the sidelines near the Memphis bench. Coach Jay Triano called for his "rim" play, instructing Dragan Bender to throw the ball directly at the rim. Tyson Chandler, who goes 7′ 1″, and his defender, the 6′ 9″ Brandan Wright, were the only men in the paint. The ball did make contact with the rim, and Chandler did touch the basketball while part of it was above the rim, but he controlled it enough to guide it home, dunking with both hands as time expired. Interesting play, but was it legal?

Answer on page 155

(3) In the 2018 NCAA women's tournament, Tennessee began play with a 100–60 win over Liberty. Mercedes Russell of the Lady Vols made a layup with her team up by two and 4:06 remaining in the second quarter, but the ball never came through the bottom of a very tight net. It dropped below the rim but stayed nestled at the bottom of the net. Is the basket good, or is this a jump ball situation?

Answer on pages 155–156

(4) Indiana State met Michigan State in March of 1979 for the heavily anticipated marquee matchup of the Spartans' charismatic star Magic Johnson and the Sycamores' Larry Bird, who won Player of the Year honors that season. The winner of this clash would go home national champs.

Bird averaged nearly 29 points and 15 rebounds per game on the regular season, and Johnson was good for 17.1 points and 8.4 assists each time he took to the court.

One play from the 1979 title game involving Johnson brings up the next *You're the Basketball Ref* situation. Magic made a jab step away from the basket, and Leroy Staley, the player defending him, fell for it, overplaying Johnson and allowing the MSU star to make an uncontested cut to the lane.

Taking a pass from Greg Kelser, Magic penetrated and dunked. As he neared the hoop, forward Bob Heaton slid over to play help defense on Johnson, winding up underneath the leaping Johnson. Heaton seems to have been trying to establish position, probably hoping to draw a charge, but the refs ruled he had fouled Johnson while the latter was high above the hardwood floor, in the act of dunking. They said the basket counted and sent Magic to the line to shoot two free throws.

Why wasn't this an "and-one" situation, one that could've resulted in a three-, and not a potential *four*-point play?

Answers on page 156–157

Answers on page 156–157

⑤ One controversial play from an NBA playoff game in 2018 involved LeBron James playing the lead role. The Cavs were taking on the Pacers in the opening round of the playoffs, and the game came down to its final 3.3 seconds. At that point, Victor Oladipo drove to the hoop for a reverse layup when James took to the sky and blocked the shot. Replays made it seem pretty obvious that the Cavs star had swatted the ball after it had hit the glass. The refs did not make a call.

The Pacers, who lost by a 98–95 score, watched video of the play when they went to their locker room and knew they had been robbed. Why was no official replay made during the game so that the play might have been overturned?

Answer on page 157

(6) The scene was Game 4 of the Eastern Conference Finals with the Celtics playing in Cleveland on May 21, 2018. LeBron James snared a defensive rebound and began racing down the court with one defender, Marcus Smart, ahead of him and another, Semi Ojeleye, about a step behind him.

Anticipating that James would most likely take it all the way for a bucket, Ojeleye wrapped his arms around James from behind, halting his progress. The whistle blew. What was the call?

Answer on page 157

(7) Same Celtics versus Cavs game from the 2018 playoffs. A poor pass from James to J.R. Smith nearly hit off Smith's fingers *and* off referee Eric Lewis, who was standing out of bounds. Smith somehow caught the ball before it could touch Lewis. Now, a pretty easy question—if the

basketball had touched Lewis, and had Smith then made the catch, would play continue, or would the ball be considered out of bounds?

Answer on page 157

8 While there was a crazy game that took place a long time ago, mentioned elsewhere in this book, in which a team played with (much) fewer than five players, this next somewhat similar bizarre scenario comes from November of 2017.

Alabama (No. 25) and Minnesota, ranked higher at No. 14, met at the Barclays Center Classic in Brooklyn, where a scuffle broke out. The entire Bama bench went onto the court, but no Golden Gopher left his bench. None of the Alabama bench players participated in the fracas, though, and no punches were thrown. What punishment, if any, was dished out?

Answer on page 158

9 Another question from that same game. More chaos came soon when, at the 11:37 mark, Alabama was down to four players after Dazon Ingram fouled out. Under current NCAA rules, what should happen at that point? a) the game moves on after a technical foul is assessed against Alabama; b) the game is forfeited to Minnesota; c) play on, no penalty for playing with four men.

Answer on page 158

Hypothetical question: would NCAA rules permit a team to play with just two men left on the court? With one?

Answer on page 158

11 In the 1983 NCAA tournament semifinals in the Pit in Albuquerque, New Mexico, Houston was matched up against Louisville. The No. 1 Cougars (29–2 on the season) were led by Hakeem Olajuwon, Clyde Drexler, and Michael Young; this was the famous, high-flying Phi Slama Jama group. The Cardinals, No. 2 in the nation, featured Lancaster Gordon, Milt Wagner, and Charles Jones, along with Rodney and Scooter McCray. Houston entered the game owning the longest win streak in the country at 25 games, and Louisville was on a roll, too, with 16 consecutive victories to their credit.

With the Cardinals up by four, Scooter McCray picked off a pass from Alvin Franklin and began to dribble down the sideline near the Houston bench. There, clutching his omnipresent, trademark red polka-dot towel, stood Cougars coach Guy Lewis. As McCray shot by him, a disgusted Lewis threw his towel, which hit McCray, then fluttered onto the floor.

If you were the ref, would you have: a) blown the whistle and had the towel removed so nobody could slip on it and possibly get hurt?; b) let play continue until a dead ball occurred and then have the towel taken away?; c) let play continue until it ended and then called a technical foul on Lewis?; d) immediately T'd Lewis up?

Answer on page 159

12 On the first of March in 2018, the No. 1 Virginia Cavaliers traveled to Louisville to face the Cardinals. The host team seemed on the verge of an upset of the 26–2 Cavaliers, leading by a seemingly insurmountable four points with just 5.8 seconds left on the clock.

However, Ty Jerome was fouled in the act of shooting a three-pointer, a monumental defensive blunder, and Jerome made two foul shots. The lead was sliced to two, but with precious little time left in the game. On the third shot, Virginia was guilty of a lane violation, and Louisville took possession with a mere nine-tenths of a second to go. Game over—or was it? Deng Adel then ran the baseline in order to find a teammate to inbound the ball to. The ref's whistle blew. Why?

Answer on page 159

MIKE KRZYZEWSKI

ANSWERS

(1) Absolutely. The refs did go to the replay and verified what they probably already knew, that Torres wasn't making a play on, say, the ball and certainly deserved to be slapped with a flagrant 1 foul for mugging Bagley. Any unnecessary or excessive contact as well as any holding or pushing a player from behind to stop a score will result in a flagrant foul being called.

Bagley didn't connect on either of his two free throws, but in the long run, it didn't matter, as Duke won by 18.

(2) This is legal even though Chandler first touched the ball while it was partially within the cylinder. While a team can't shoot the ball directly *into* the hoop on an inbound pass, there is no offensive goaltending on the play here. Again, the play would have been illegal *if* the ball had gone straight through the rim without Chandler touching it.

The obscure rule states no goaltending or basket interference can be called on this play, so it is treated like "an ordinary throw-in and anyone may attempt to gain possession of the ball without penalty." Triano, who had long known about the loophole and had waited 15 or so years to unveil the play, had done his research, and it paid off.

(3) The basket should have counted under the rules, but the officials, after a long review, somehow got this one

155

wrong. The women's rulebook states a basket counts any-time the ball "remains in or passes through the basket." The ball certainly did pass through the rim, and even if the definition of the basket is meant to include the net itself, the ball did remain in the net—so, either way, Tennessee was robbed of the field goal (plus Russell was fouled on the play). Russell did go to the line and made two free throws, but she was denied a chance to cash in on a three-point play.

Also, another thought to be considered: a few seconds after the ball got trapped in the net, a Liberty player smacked the ball up and over the rim, back onto the court. An article by Henry Bushnell on Yahoo Sports pointed out that even if the officials were figuring the basket didn't count and the ball was still live while it was dangling in the net, then shouldn't the officials have called goaltending on the Liberty player who batted the ball to free it?

(4) The officials called this an airborne foul, and a visibly upset Johnson, who acted as if he had been undercut on the play, certainly agreed. Under the rules, the basket counted, and two shots were awarded. The refs were correct.

This scenario wound up with Johnson completing a four-point play, as he not only made his shot from the field, but also sank both of his free throws. Not long before this play, Bird had drawn his team to within six points, and momentum seemed to possibly be swinging the Sycamores' way. However, when Johnson concluded his four-point play to open up a 61–50 lead, many believed they had just witnessed the pivotal point in the contest.

The game ended with the much deeper Spartan team maintaining their advantage and putting ISU away, 75–64. Johnson led all players with 24 points to go with his five assists, and Kelser topped all players with nine assists. Bird's 13 boards led all players, and his 19 points led Indiana State.

(5) James got away with goaltending. The NBA's report of officiated events that take place in games that are at or within three points during the final 2:00 states that goaltending should have been called. The key to the play was simple: with no whistle blown on the play, no review of the play was permitted.

(6) Send James to the line for two shots. However, if you guessed it was an intentional foul and the Cavs would retain the ball, you're wrong. That would actually be the correct call under international rules, but because Smart was between James and the basket, the Cavs star had no clear path to the hoop, and the NBA declares that while players in such a situation do get their two shots, this is not an intentional foul.

(7) The ball would be dead once it touched the out-of-bounds Lewis. Turnover.

(8) Officials ejected the entire Crimson Tide bench, seven players, for going onto the court, but assigned no additional penalty because the seven men didn't actually get involved in the action. So, with 13:39 to play in the game, Alabama literally had no bench at all.

(9) c) The game went on, and with another twist. Almost exactly one minute later, with 10:41 to go in the game, Alabama's John Petty left the game with an ankle injury. Reduced to playing with three men—Galin Smith, Ricky Norris, and Collin Sexton—the Crimson Tide somehow outscored their opponents, 30–22, down the stretch. How's that for 3-on-5 basketball?! Stunningly, they cut their deficit to a mere three points but wound up losing, 89–84, despite going on a 26–16 run against all odds.

A key to the Alabama shorthanded comeback attempt was Sexton, who set a school record for a freshman with his 40 points on the night.

(10) Yes, a college game can continue with just two players when all of the other players on that team are unable to play or are not eligible to play. As for going on with just one man, well, Rule 3, Section 1, Article 3 reads like this: "When there is only one player participating for a team, that team shall forfeit unless the referee believes that both teams have an opportunity to win." That certainly seems like an odd judgment call to have to make.

(11) d) The ref stopped play right away and called a technical foul on the Houston coach. On a much less serious scale than Ohio State football coach Woody Hayes, Lewis was guilty of interfering with an opponent. During the 1978 Gator Bowl, an utterly disgruntled and out-of-control Hayes actually slugged Clemson nose guard Charlie Bauman after he had intercepted a Buckeye pass and returned it near the Buckeye bench. That action soon led to Hayes getting fired. Compared to what Hayes did, Lewis's actions were minor but he did hurt his team, as his temper tantrum helped Louisville build a five-point lead at the half.

It wound up not mattering at all. Houston stormed back, wearing down Louisville, 94–81, and advancing to the championship game. They would not continue their torrid win streak, though. North Carolina State nipped them, 54–52, on the famous rebound and ensuing buzzer-beating dunk by Lorenzo Charles off a missed Dereck Whittenburg shot.

(12) In such a situation, after the lane infraction, running with the ball is a traveling violation, and the ball went back to Virginia. With under a second left on the clock, the Cavaliers, who had trailed by 13 at one point in the second half, desperately had to get a shot off. Freshman De'Andre Hunter managed to do so, banking in a three-pointer right at the buzzer to seal a stunning 67–66 comeback win.

Jerome wound up the game's high scorer with 21, and the unfortunate Adel led Louisville with 18.

SO YOU STILL WANT TO BE A REF?

B asketball officials lead an oncourt life of pressure, as intense as a smothering full-court press. Being a basketball official is, in numerous ways, as demanding as, for instance, umpiring baseball. Both jobs are highly demanding—as the classic line of major league umpire Ed Runge goes, "It's the only occupation where a man has to be perfect the first day on the job and then improve over the years." NBA ref Earl Strom concurred, cognizant that his job was thankless. "Officiating," he opined, "is the only occupation in the world where the highest accolade is silence."

Refs are easy targets and often become scapegoats. In February 2012, Ohio State sophomore star Jared Sullinger blamed a slump he was languishing through, including an eight-point, six-rebound off night against Wisconsin, on—who else—the refs. He told *Plain Dealer* writer Doug Lesmerises that he had to work on not thinking about the referees in order to get back on track. Lesmerises wrote that Sullinger believed officials were calling him for fouls "on defense that his defenders then weren't getting called for while guarding him." Playing too often with four fouls, Sullinger conceded that "It's strictly mental" and that he was "constantly worried about the refs instead of how I was supposed to play."

Refs must be able to handle the pressure and expectations of perfection, along with coping with ceaseless and merciless

bellowing from coaches and fans, seemingly endless contro-
versy, brutal travel schedules, being away from family for long
periods of time, and so much more.

Furthermore, contrary to what some ill-informed fans
might think, referees don't simply pull up to an arena's parking
lot 10 minutes before a game is scheduled to start, hop out of
their car, blithely stroll into the building, and toss the ball in
the air for the opening tipoff. They have many duties before,
during, and even after games. A few simple examples from the
rulebook include:

1) Inspecting and approving "all equipment, including court,
baskets, balls, backboards, timers, and scorer's equipment."

2) Checking the game balls "to see they are properly
inflated. The recommended ball pressure should be between
7 1/2 and 8 1/2 pounds."

3) Reporting to the Commissioner "any atypical or unique
incident, flagrant foul, punching foul, fighting . . ."

Few fans think about it, but Julius Erving once observed
that, "The real good official knows what's important to call. Professional basketball is part of the entertainment business, but
the first order of business is allowing the play to be at its highest level. An official can encourage that, or he can destroy it."

That belief holds true even at the high school level. Mark
Pena noted that there is a difference between the letter of the
law and "the spirit of the game—what we're trying to do is let
kids play through things so that we don't end up with a foul
shooting contest."

Being a ref is constantly living a no-win existence on the
court. Take for example the argument that the way a ref calls a

REFEREE JOE DEROSA, TALKING WITH ASSISTANT COACH ANDY GREER

game should vary when the game winds down to its final seconds. Jeff Eisenberg wrote a piece for Yahoo! Sports, discussing this very matter. Some fans and coaches contend a rule is a rule and refs should rigidly enforce the rulebook, spotting and calling infractions consistently—if something was a violation shortly after the opening tip, it should be a violation in the game's deciding moments. Others, however, argue that a game's final outcome should be a result more of players' performances and not referees' calls. These people, wrote Eisenberg, "prefer to see referees make a game-changing call only when egregiously necessary."

Coaches tend to believe that if they "work" the officials, vociferously arguing many calls, a ref will perhaps try to even things out or even make up for a bad call by later giving the coach a "makeup" call. In the 2012 NCAA Tournament, Louisville's Rick Pitino was convinced his coaching counterpart, Florida's Billy Donovan, was employing such tactics. Early on in the second half, Donovan rode the refs hard during a timeout. Shortly after play resumed, the refs called a foul on Pitino's Cardinals, prompting him to bellow, "He [Donovan] called that. Why don't you just give him a whistle?" Such moments frequently cause refs to either pretend to be deaf or hit a coach with a technical foul. Either way, the ref doesn't exactly feel good about the situation.

In an early era of the NBA, in a rougher, less sophisticated time than now, threats against refs made by players were not unheard of. After referee Pete D'Ambrosio called a foul on Richie Guerin, the player snarled, "I'll get you outside." Shortly after that, Guerin again spouted off, "I'll punch your head off."

Naturally, D'Ambrosio hit him up with a "T," but when he later told his partner Sid Borgia about the threat, Borgia seemed almost blasé: "Yeah, Guerin said the same thing to me once."

Once, as Joe Gushue walked off the court after working a game in Syracuse, a fan reached out and smacked his head with a newspaper. Gushue turned to a police officer working crowd control that night, looking for support. "Did you see that?" he asked. The officer replied, "The way you called the game, no one saw anything."

When Bill Russell was asked for his opinion on the concept of having women for referees, he replied that he was all for it because, as he put it, "Incompetence should not be confined to one sex." Obviously, refs get little sympathy or understanding outside their circle of peers.

Of course, some refs take matters into their own fists. Borgia was working a Boston-Syracuse game in the old Syracuse War Memorial Auditorium, and, after taking a heap of abuse from a fan, he decided, like Popeye, "That's all I can stands, I can't stands no more," and he went into the stands, located the fan, and belted him. Havoc ensued as fights broke out seemingly everywhere (and this was in 1959, long before Ron Artest made his fiasco of a foray into the stands to take on fans). When things calmed down, Boston coach Red Auerbach gazed over at the bloody fan, then turned to Borgia. "That was the only damn good thing you did all night."

One way for basketball officials to put up with such a tough existence is by having a good sense of humor. Veteran basketball ref Joey Crawford, son of major league ump Shag (from 1956 to 1975) and brother of big-league umpire

Jerry (1976–2000), once called a foul on Stojko Vrankovic. When he walked over to the scorers' table to announce it, he mentally fumbled, then came out with, "Loose ball on whatever the hell his name is."

Often, though, the humor involving referees is negative and/or sarcastic, but hearing such jokes without taking them personally or without seeking retribution is part of the official's job—a ref with "rabbit ears" won't last too long, and, usually, yes *usually*, the jokes aren't meant to be taken too seriously. Take the time Kevin Loughery was coaching the hapless New York Nets. During a game that was destined to become their 13th loss in a row, Loughery teased referees Walter Rooney and Earl Strom over a call. "Hey," shouted out the frustrated, but witty coach, "you guys are worse than we are."

Bob Conibear, who once coached Bowling Green, made a comment that went beyond being one of ridicule—his remark was, if taken seriously, rather vicious. After losing a tight game, no doubt in his mind due to the refs, he told the press the next day that he had a dream that he was "on a safari in Africa and killed every zebra I saw."

Make no mistake, nowadays, severe criticism of officiating can be relatively costly. Take just one rather basic example (of *many* that occur in the NBA) from March of 2012. Chicago Bulls star Derrick Rose's negative comments about refs led to the league fining him $25,000. Of course, that amount was considerably less than 1 percent of Rose's salary, but the fine is the NBA's way of saying that they simply won't ignore verbal abuse of their referees.

Speaking of salary, when the league began in 1946, the average pay for a player was $4,500 per season, so you can imagine the meager amount of money refs made back then. At one point, they earned as little as $30 per game. By 1983, NBA officials were paid between $18,146 and $78,259 for a season's work. It took a long time before NBA referees were making a decent living, but in recent years, that has changed, and nowadays they do earn a hefty chunk of cash. By 2009—for instance—NBA "entry-level referees" were earning $150,000 per year "according to information released by the league." The NBA's Referees Association, disagreeing with that figure, said the correct salary was $91,000.

No matter the pay, the job has never been easy. It wasn't until the 1988–1989 season that the NBA recognized the fact that trying to watch and handle ten athletic men—often large and/or mercury-quick on a basketball court—was no easy task for two officials. That season, help in the form of a third ref finally came along.

Tommy Canterbury, who coached the men's basketball team at Centenary, once said something that was meant to be a humorous criticism of refs but actually came off as a compliment. "The trouble with officials," he stated, "is they just don't care who wins."

How true. For the most part, nobody questions the integrity of referees. Players' integrity, yes, at certain times in basketball history, but refs, not so much. No, we're not forgetting about, for example, the scandal involving former NBA referee Tim Donaghy, and, in defense of the league, the NBA did react by revamping their rules on gambling.

NBA REFEREES (FROM LEFT TO RIGHT) TONY BROTHERS, HAYWOODE WORKMAN, AND MICHAEL SMITH

By way of background on the subject of hoop scandals, basketball's version of baseball's most salient infamy that took place back in 1919 when the Chicago White Sox threw the World Series, it should be noted that between the years 1947 and 1950, there were 86 college games played that were known to be fixed. Unlike the Black Sox incident, the gambling in basketball was widespread—32 players, but absolutely no referees, were found to be involved as the wave of point-shaving notoriety rocked such programs as Long Island University, Bradley, and City College of New York, the only team ever to win both the National Invitation Tournament and the NCAA Tournament in the same year.

On a much smaller scale involving a team being given an advantage, you'll always have some discontented people claiming a ref is a "homer," but as Mark Pena stated, "When you're out on the floor, everything is so instinctive and so split second—I don't know, if somebody can blatantly do that [consciously give calls to the home team], God bless them because I know I can't. I call the game one way, but when I blow my whistle, it's instinctive—I don't have time to think, 'Well, wait a minute, he's from the home team, I can't call it on him.'"

Then there are the cases in which an individual player seems to be getting an edge in the eyes of a fan or even, for instance, an NBA rookie who may grumble and contend refs give breaks to veterans, especially the superstars of the game. Well let's face it, sometimes in sports, as in life, there is a disparity between the way one thinks things *should* be done and how things actually *are* done. Most rookies accept the NBA facts of life. In 1992, Antonio Harvey—then a rookie with the

Los Angeles Lakers—said he understood that referees "respect guys who have proven they can last and deserve to get breaks on calls. They make you prove you deserve respect on the court. If you play hard and don't walk around with a chip on your shoulder, they'll treat you with respect."

The same probably holds true for referees—the ones who work hard and don't hold a grudge will gain respect. Even then, many other ingredients are required to excel as a ref including, just to name a few, the guts to make tough calls, getting and staying in top physical shape, a willingness to listen and be fair while at the same time being firm, and a thorough knowledge and understanding of a veritable tome of rules.

Despite all of the demands and the negative aspects of being a ref, the bottom line concerning the occupation may ultimately be quite simple—at least according to longtime referee Ed T. Rush: "It is, in my opinion, the best job in sports. You're on the court, you're part of the game, you're connected to the game. . . . Every night there is something different. . . . The compensation is very good and there is a long vacation."

Thus, for the elite who can tolerate the negatives and optimistically see so many positives, a lifetime of wearing stripes and blowing a whistle can truly be rewarding on many levels including self-satisfaction. As Alex Sachare wrote, "Like the athletes they officiate, NBA referees are the best in the world."

PAT RILEY

CAN YOU BE A REF?

Now that you've finished this book and learned a bit of knowledge about the sport, let's see how well you would do during a game. Below are several images of referee hand signals. Match the action to the correct call.

A

1   Holding

B

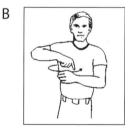

2   Personal Foul

C

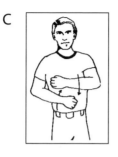

3 Basket Interference

D

4 Jump Ball

E

5 Traveling

---

*Officials' hand signals are courtesy of the book, *Basketball Made Simple: A Spectator's Guide*, pgs. 124–127 (www.fristbasesports.com)

*1-E ,2-D ,3-C ,4-B ,5-A

A

1   No Basket

B

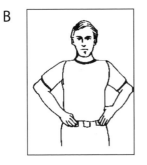

2   20-Second Time Out

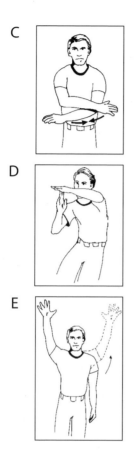

C

D

E

3   3-Point Field Goal

4   Blocking Foul

5   Technical Foul

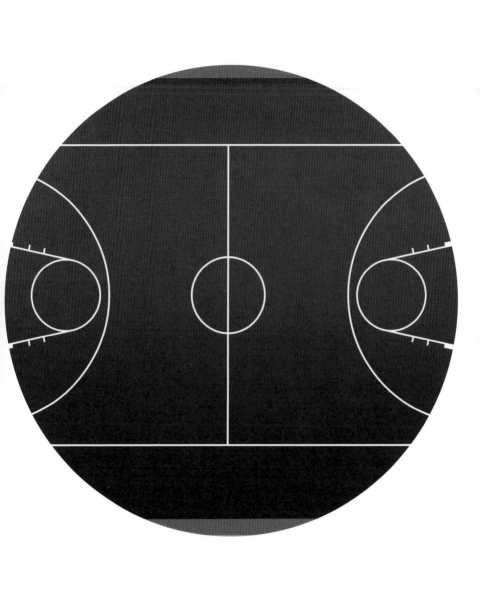

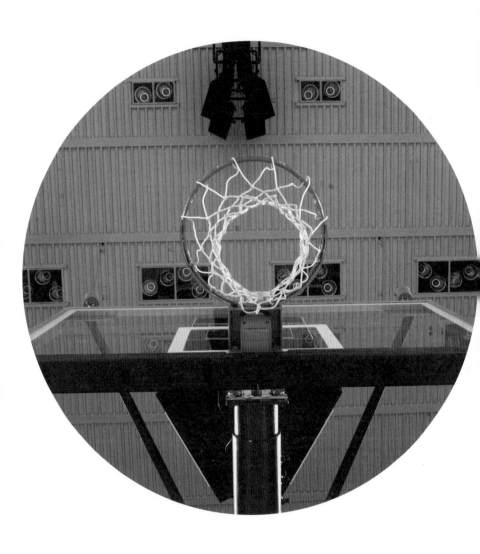

QUIZZES FOR THE BASKETBALL JUNKIE

Now that you've mastered the questions in this book and know your referee hand signals, let's see how you do with general basketball knowledge. Rather than giving you layups, these quizzes will test not only your overall NBA IQ, but how closely you follow the sport. Don't get discouraged if you cannot figure out all the answers, as even we cheated when putting this together!

NICKNAMES

Since the beginning of basketball, nicknames have gone hand-in-hand with the game. Whether it's a self-given one or something their grandmother used to call them, these names follow players throughout their careers. Now you may think that the first couple of pages are easy, but it'll only get harder as you continue on. Good luck!

1.	Agent Zero	A. Kevin Garnett
2.	Black Mamba	B. Allen Iverson
3.	Sir Charles	C. Dennis Rodman
4.	Muggsy	D. Gilbert Arenas
5.	The Birdman	E. Tyrone Bogues
6.	The Truth	F. Kobe Bryant
7.	The Answer	G. Paul Pierce
8.	The Worm	H. Chris Anderson
9.	Mr. Big Shot	I. Charles Barkley
10.	The Big Ticket	J. Chauncey Billups

1.	The Jet	A. Karl Malone
2.	Diesel	B. Jerome Williams
3.	Tiny	C. Gary Payton
4.	The Glove	D. Phil Jackson
5.	The Zen Master	E. Ronald Jones
6.	Junkyard Dog	F. Rick Smitts
7.	Speedy	G. Craig Claxton
8.	Dunking Dutchman	H. Kenny Smith
9.	The Mailman	I. Shaquille O'Neal
10.	Popeye	J. Nate Archibald

1.	The Dream	A.	Ervin Johnson
2.	Pistol Pete	B.	George Gervin
3.	The Hick from French Lick	C.	Amar'e Stoudemire
4.	STAT	D.	Hakeem Olajuwon
5.	Big O	E.	Glenn Rivers
6.	Dr. J	F.	Julius Erving
7.	Doc	G.	Pete Maravich
8.	Magic	H.	Oscar Robinson
9.	The Pearl	I.	Larry Bird
10.	Iceman	J.	Earl Monroe

1. The Admiral   A. Glenn Robinson

2. CP3   B. Robert Horry

3. Big Ben   C. Earl Boynkins

4. The Candy Man   D. Jerry West

5. Big Shot Bob   E. Dominique Wilkins

6. Flash   F. Chris Paul

7. The Squirrel   G. David Robinson

8. The Logo   H. Ben Wallace

9. Big Dog   I. Lamar Odom

10. The Human Highlight Reel   J. Dwayne Wade

1. Big Country

A. Walt Frazier

2. The X-Man

B. LeBron James

3. AK47

C. Bryant Reeves

4. Big Baby

D. Toni Kukoc

5. King James

E. Dwight Howard

6. Clyde the Glide

F. Glen Davis

7. Clyde

G. Rafer Alston

8. The Pink Panther

H. Xavier McDaniel

9. Superman

I. Andrei Kirilenko

10. Skip To My Lou

J. Clyde Drexler

50 GREATEST PLAYERS IN NBA HISTORY

In 1996, for the 50th anniversary of the NBA, former players, coaches, and media members voted on the 50 Greatest Players in NBA history. They were announced by Commissioner David Stern on October 29, 1996. While we cannot personally time you, see how many of the 50 you can name in ten minutes. But remember, no cheating!

1. _____

2. _____

3. _____

4. _____

5. _____

6. _____

7. _____

8. _____

9. _____

10. _____

11. _____

12. _____

13. _____

14. _____

15. _____

16. _____

17. _____

18. _____

19. _____

20. _____

21. _____

22. _____

23. _____

24. _____

25. _____

26. _____

27. _____

28. _____

29. _____

30. _____

31. _____

32. _____

33. _____

34. _____

35. _____

36. _____

37. _____

38. _____

39. _____

40. _____

41. _____

42. _____

43. _____

44. _____

45. _____

46. _____

47. _____

48. _____

49. _____

50. _____

1. Kareem Abdul-Jabbar

2. Nate Archibald

3. Paul Arizin

4. Charles Barkley

5. Rick Barry

6. Elgin Baylor

7. Dave Bing

8. Larry Bird

9. Wilt Chamberlain

10. Bob Cousy

11. Dave Cowens

12. Billy Cunningham

13. Dave DeBusschere

14. Clyde Drexler

15. Julius Erving

16. Patrick Ewing

17. Walt Frazier

18. George Gervin

19. Hal Greer

20. John Havlicek

21. Elvin Hayes

22. Magic Johnson

23. Sam Jones

24. Michael Jordan

25. Jerry Lucas

26. Karl Malone

27. Moses Malone

28. Pete Maravich

29. Kevin McHale

30. George Mikan

31. Earl Monroe

32. Hakeem Olajuwon

33. Shaquille O'Neal

34. Robert Parish

35. Bob Pettit

36. Scottie Pippen

37. Willis Reed

38. Oscar Robertson

39. David Robinson

40. Bill Russell

41. Dolph Schayes

42. Bill Sharman

43. John Stockton

44. Isiah Thomas

45. Nate Thurmond

46. Wes Unseld

47. Bill Walton

48. Jerry West

49. Lenny Wilkens

50. James Worthy

NBA TEAMS

There are 30 NBA teams (through 2018) in the East and West, with three conferences in each (Atlantic, Central, and Southeast in the East and Northwest, Pacific, and Southwest in the West). The first part of this quiz might not be too difficult, but the second part is. Give yourself ten minutes and name all 30 NBA teams. After that, take an additional five minutes and name the original 11 NBA teams that began in 1946.

East

Atlantic	Central	Southeast

West

Northwest	Pacific	Southwest

Original 11 NBA Teams

East

Atlantic	Central	Southeast
Boston Celtics	Chicago Bulls	Atlanta Hawks
Brooklyn Nets	Cleveland Cavaliers	Charlotte Hornets
New York Knicks	Detroit Pistons	Miami Heat
Philadelphia 76ers	Indiana Pacers	Orlando Magic
Toronto Raptors	Milwaukee Bucks	Washington Wizards

West

Northwest	Pacific	Southwest
Denver Nuggets	Golden State Warriors	Dallas Mavericks
Minnesota Timberwolves	Los Angeles Clippers	Houston Rockets
Oklahoma City Thunder	Los Angeles Lakers	Memphis Grizzles
Portland Trail Blazers	Phoenix Suns	New Orleans Pelicans
Utah Jazz	Sacramento Kings	San Antonio Spurs

Original 11 NBA Teams

Boston Celtics	Chicago Stags	Cleveland Rebels
Detroit Falcons	New York Knickerbockers	Philadelphia Warriors
Pittsburgh Ironmen	Providence Steamrollers	St. Louis Bombers
Toronto Huskies		Washington Capitols

ACKNOWLEDGMENTS

Thanks go out to my former Skyhorse editor, Mark Weinstein, who nurtured me through the first two of the three books I've now done on sports, sports officials (be they umpires or referees), and rules—*You're the Umpire, You're the Ref* (Football), and now this book. Also, a thank-you is in order to Jay Cassell, my editor on this particular title, and to Jason Katzman, an editor at Skyhorse, for his invaluable input as well. Additionally, my thanks to Skyhorse's Julie Ganz for all the work she put into the making of this book. A special thanks to my sons, Sean and Scott Stewart, for their help on this book, as well.

Finally, a big thank-you for the people I interviewed as I worked on *You're the Basketball Ref*, as well as those who helped out in other ways to make my job easier: Pete Carbonaro, Greg Peltz, and Mark Pena.

ABOUT THE AUTHOR

Wayne Stewart was born and raised in Donora, Pennsylvania, a town that has produced a handful of big league baseball players and a slew of other sports standouts, a remarkable feat, considering the size of the town known as "The Home of the Champions." The stars include luminaries such as Hall of Fame baseball player Stan Musial and the father-son Griffeys, as well as a man who once led the NFL in rushing, "Deacon" Dan Towler.

Stewart was a member of the same Donora High School baseball team as Ken Griffey, Sr. Stewart now lives in Amherst, Ohio, a Cleveland suburb, with his wife, Nancy. They have two sons, Sean and Scott, and one grandchild, Nathan.

Stewart has covered the sports world since 1978 and has written over 500 articles for publications such as *Baseball Digest*, *USA Today/Baseball Weekly*, *Boys' Life*, and Beckett Publications. He has written for several newspapers in the Cleveland area and has hosted a call-in sports talk show, a pregame show for Cleveland Indians broadcasts, and a pregame show leading into Notre Dame football games—all for a radio station in Lorain, Ohio. Furthermore, Stewart has appeared as a baseball expert/historian on Cleveland's FOX 8 and on an ESPN Classic television special on Bob Feller. A few of his previous books include a biography of Musial, *Stan the Man: The Life and Times of Stan Musial*, *Baseball Dads*, *You're the Umpire, You're the Ref* (Football), *Hitting Secrets of the Pros*, *Pitching Secrets of the Pros*, *The Little Giant Book of Basketball Facts*, and *Babe Ruth: A Biography*. To learn more about Stewart and his books, go to waynestewartonsports.blog

SOURCES

Author Interviews
Pete Carbonaro
Antonio Harvey
Greg Peltz
Mark Pena

Books
1001 Stupid Sports Quotes edited by Randy Howe
Basketball's Most Wanted II by David L. Hudson, Jr.
ESPN College Basketball Encyclopedia by the editors of ESPN
The Little Giant Book of Basketball Facts by Wayne Stewart
The Norm Hitzges Historical Sports Almanac by Norm Hitzges
The Official NBA Encyclopedia edited by Jan Hubbard
The Sports 100 by Brad Herzog
Sportswit by Lee Green
The 25 Greatest Centers of All Time by Mark Heisler
Veeck as in Wreck by Bill Veeck
Wilt by Gary M. Pomerantz

Newspapers
The Associated Press for various articles
The Plain Dealer for various items including Brian Windhorst's
    "Rule Change Legalizes LeBron's 'Crab Dribble,'" from
    October 18, 2009.

Magazine
Basketball Digest

Websites
http://www.aolnews.com/2009/09/29/tip-off-timer
-chamberlain-and-dantleys-record-28-free-throws/
http://aol.sportingnews.com/ncaa-basketball/story
/2011-03-31/lew-alcindor-set-the-tone-for-the-1967
-ucla-bruins
http://auburnpub.com/sports/local/close-call-syracuse
-survives-north-carolina-asheville-s-upset-bid
/article_51411b44-6f16-11e1-9f4b-001871e3ce6c.html
http://www.ballhistory.com/basketball.htm
http://www.basketball-reference.com
http://bleacherreport.com/articles/553751-nba-rituals-the
-top-10-free-throw-shooting-routines-or-lack-of-of-all
-time#/articles/553751-nba-rituals-the-top-10-free-throw
-shooting-routines-or-lack-of-of-all-time
http://www.cbc.ca/news/story/2008/05/07/f-olympics
-basketball-essentials.html
http://www.CBSSports.com
http://www.enquirer.com/editions/2003/03/17/spt
_wwwsptsnba17.html
http://www.fairportbasketball.com/2002/tab/main/links
/bbquotes_funny.htm
http://www.firstbasesports.com
http://www.hickoksports.com/biograph/russellbill.shtml
http://www.highschoolrivals.com

http://hoopedia.nba.com/index.php?title=NBA_Rules
    _History_1946-1980

http://hoopedia.nba.com/index.php?title=NBA_Rules
    _History_1980-Present

http://www.huffingtonpost.com/2011/01/28/inbounds-pass
    -basket-sacopee-valley_n_815500.html

http://www.ihoops.com/training-room/officials/officials
    -guide-secction-15-seven-basketball-rules-myths.htm

http://inventors.about.com/library/inventors/blbasketball
    _rules.htm

http://www.livestrong.com/article/345716-evolution-of-basketball/

http://www.livestrong.com/article/389245-basketball-game
    -clock-rules/

http://msn.foxsports.com/nba/story/Dwight-Howard-breaks
    -Wilt-Chamberlain-free-throw-record-as-Orlando-Magic
    -beat-Golden-State-Warriors-011212?gt1=39002

http://www.nba.com/analysis/rules

http://www.nba.com/history/dreamT_moments.html

http://www.nba.com/nba101/misunderstood_0708.html

http://nbahoopsonline.com/History/Leagues/NBA
    /pointsingame.html

http://nba-point-forward.si.com/2011/04/07/on-the-dwight
    -howard-ree-throw-everyone-is-wrong-except-gerald
    -henderson/

http://www.nbsashooters.com/records

http://www.ncaapublications.com/productdownloads/BR13
    .pdf

http://www.negativedunkalectics.com/2011/05/shooting-at
    -wrong-basket-nba-rulebook.html

http://www.nfhs.org

http://www.nytimes.com/2012/03/16/sports/ncaabasketball
/2012-ncaa-tournament-syracuse-avoids-upset-by-no-16
-unc-asheville.html?_r=1

http://osaabasketball.arbitersports.com/Groups/105990
/Library/files/GoalTendingandBasketballInterference.pdf

http://www.referee.com/more/Samples/non_subscribers0106
/free_admin.html

http://sports.espn.go.com/espn/classic/news/story?page
=add_Francis_Bevo

http://sports.espn.go.com/nba/news/story?id=3079309

http://www.sports-reference.com/cbb/seasons/2007.html

http://sports.yahoo.com/blogs/ncaab-the-dagger/alabama
-fan-face-sign-instant-internet-hit-172350668.html

http://sports.yahoo.com/blogs/ncaab-the-dagger/costly-lane
-violation-thwarts-notre-dame-comeback-bid-055247953
.html

http://www.usabasketball.com/mens/national/moly_1972.html

Photos

Mauer, Washington, Javie, pg. 3, courtesy of Keith Allison

Chris Paul, pg. 13, courtesy of Keith Allison

Wilt Chamberlain, pg. 17, courtesy of AP Images

Referee Matt Boland, pg. 27, courtesy of AP Images

Larry Bird and Kareem Abdul-Jabbar, pg. 30, courtesy of AP
Images

Dwight Howard, pg. 35, courtesy of Keith Allison

NBA Referees Instant Replay, pg. 61, courtesy of Keith Allison

Jack Blankenship, pg. 72, courtesy of AP Images

SOURCES

Duke vs. North Carolina, pg. 74, courtesy of Bluedog 423
(Wikimedia Commons)

Anthony Davis, pg. 82, courtesy of Ian McCormick

Chris Webber, pg. 85, courtesy of AP Images

Lew Alcindor, pg. 100, courtesy of By New York World-
Telegram and the Sun staff photographer (Wikimedia
Commons)

Brittney Griner, pg. 124, courtesy of AP Images

David Robinson, pg. 127, courtesy of Ken Hackman, U.S. Air
Force (Wikimedia Commons)

Jump Ball, pg. 130, courtesy of AP Images

Referee Shelly Mangrum, pg. 132, courtesy of AP Images

Karima Christmas, pg. 139, courtesy of Keith Allison

USA Basketball Coach Chuck Daly, pg. 144, courtesy of AP
Images

Mercedes Russell, pg. 146, courtesy of AP Images

Mike Krzyzewski, pg. 154, courtesy of AP Images

Referee Joe DeRosa, pg. 163, courtesy of Keith Allison

NBA Referees Meeting, pg. 168, courtesy of Keith Allison

Pat Riley, pg. 171, courtesy of AP Images